Camping
Tennessee

Help Us Keep This Guide Up to Date

Every effort has been made by the author and editors to make this guide as accurate and useful as possible. However, many things can change after a guide is published—trails are rerouted, regulations change, techniques evolve, facilities come under new management, etc.

We would love to hear from you concerning your experiences with this guide and how you feel it could be improved and kept up to date. While we may not be able to respond to all comments and suggestions, we'll take them to heart and we'll also make certain to share them with the author. Please send your comments and suggestions to the following address:

The Globe Pequot Press
Reader Response/Editorial Department
P.O. Box 480
Guilford, CT 06437

Or you may e-mail us at:

editorial@GlobePequot.com

Thanks for your input, and happy travels!

A **FALCON** GUIDE ®

Camping
Tennessee

Harold R. Stinnette

FALCON®

GUILFORD, CONNECTICUT
HELENA, MONTANA
AN IMPRINT OF THE GLOBE PEQUOT PRESS

A FALCON GUIDE ®

All interior photos by the author.
Maps created by Jim Miller/ Fennana Design © The Globe Pequot Press

ISSN 1547-8750
ISBN 0-7627-2455-2

Manufactured in the United States of America
First Edition/First Printing

Contents

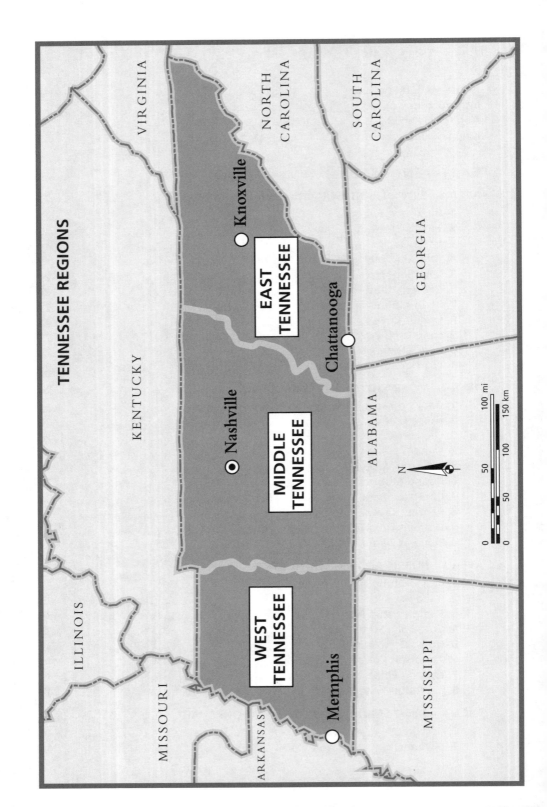

TENNESSEE REGIONS

WEST TENNESSEE

Acknowledgments

I would first like to acknowledge my wife, Donna, for her patience, encouragement, and companionship on the many outings to research this book. Without her support this project would not have been possible. I would also like to thank my parents for their company while exploring Tennessee. Thank you to all my friends for their encouragement and constant questions about "When is that book coming out?" The people I talked with at each campground are too numerous to list, but I do want to thank each of them for their help and the information they provided. I am especially grateful to the park rangers, campground staff, and campground hosts across the state. You all do an incredible job. Thank you.

Introduction

Just mentioning the name "Tennessee" brings many thoughts and words to mind: Smoky Mountains, Tennessee River, country music, Memphis Blues, Elvis Presley, Appalachia, volunteers. These words and phrases really don't describe Tennessee but merely hint at the diversity of this great state. In fact, it may be the word "diversity" that best describes Tennessee. Tennessee's diversity is found in its people, landscape, climate, culture, and music. Its music is carried in the hearts of its people—whether that music is mountain bluegrass, Nashville country, or Memphis blues depends on what part of the state you're in. The diversity of its people stretches from the folks who developed moonshine to the folks who worked on developing the atomic bomb. Now *that's* diversity!

One aspect of Tennessee that has been brought to my attention many times over the years is how friendly, open, and sincere its people are. A visit to Tennessee is like a visit home—you're always welcome. Several years ago, Tennessee Tourism used the slogan "Tennessee Feels Good to Me." This really said it all, because it is the friendly folks of this state who make it feel like home. Tennessee has four major cities—Nashville, Knoxville, Memphis, and Chattanooga—all of which are metropolitan areas with the feel of what I term "large small towns." Although they are larger cities, the people who live there still retain that small-town openness and charm.

Another way of seeing Tennessee's diversity is in its landscape. East Tennessee is a land of green mountain peaks and great valleys, rushing mountain streams and plummeting waterfalls. There is more national park and national forest land in East Tennessee than anywhere else in the state. Both of these lands make up the entire border between Tennessee and North Carolina. Middle Tennessee is a land of softly rolling hills and deep hollows and some of the most picturesque lakes in the state. Middle Tennessee is also famous for the Tennessee Walking Horse farms that grace the landscape with their green pastures. West Tennessee is a broad, flat landscape where cotton and agriculture are king. It's a wide-open landscape that spreads out to the Mississippi River. The landscape from East Tennessee to West Tennessee is so diversified that it is incredible to believe that all of this is one state.

The seasons of the year are yet another point of the state's diversity. Tennessee boasts a range of all four seasons. Spring and autumn are my favorite seasons, with temperatures being milder and more comfortable. Spring is a time of renewal—woodland wildflowers are blooming, and the hardwood trees are sprouting new leaves. Summer can be hot and humid; temperatures can reach the high nineties, with humidity readings not far behind. Summer is great for spending time at the lake or finding a respite from the heat in the mountains. Autumn is the season of change, with leaves turning their fall colors and preparing to drop to earth as summer heat gives way to cool autumn nights. Winter in Tennessee varies more than any other season. Winter temperatures can drop to the single digits, but fifty-degree winter days are also common. In a normal winter, snow is usually limited to a dusting of white, with maybe one or two measurable snows scattered around the state.

Upper East Tennessee mountains

This diversity is one of the key reasons Tennessee ranks so high in the nation in terms of tourism. Tennessee has become a tourist destination for both the individual looking for adventure and the family seeking quality entertainment. Each year more than thirty million people visit Tennessee to experience why "Tennessee Feels Good to Me." Why not join them?

For more information about visiting Tennessee visit:
www.tennesseeencyclopedia.net
www.state.tn.us/tourdev/regional.html

Zero-Impact Camping

A successful camping trip with family and friends can provide great memories for years to come. A *truly* successful trip has a positive outcome for both the camper and the environment. Leaving your camping area with zero impact on the environment and no detectable sign of your presence is a great compliment to your camping abilities. Zero impact doesn't just happen, however; you must prepare for it. Use the following guidelines before, during, and at the end of your camping trip to help ensure that the trip is a success for both you and the environment.

Plan for success. The fact that you are using a guidebook is a good start. Before camping in a new area, it's always a good idea to call ahead to find out weather and camping conditions. Preparing for the weather—for example, knowing that rain is in the forecast for that region—helps in planning what to take. You'll need to know if there are any special regulations for that camping area. For example, is it bear habitat? Are there any special food storage regulations? Having a plan for meals each day, and packing your food according to that plan, can minimize the amount of trash that must be disposed of. Make a packing list and double-check to make sure you don't forget any essential items—or carry things you don't need. Some campgrounds are very popular and fill early during peak seasons, so plan ahead and guarantee your site by getting to the campground early.

Camp only in designated areas. Most campgrounds have tent pads and paved RV sites. These are provided to minimize the impact on the areas around the campgrounds. Several campgrounds in Tennessee have strict rules concerning where to place tents and RVs; not adhering to these rules can result in a stern warning, a fine—or even expulsion. When hiking or even walking from the bathhouse, stay on established paths. Doing this lessens the impact of erosion and reduces the number of unauthorized trails cutting across and through campgrounds.

Pack it in; pack it out. The old camping rule "pack it in, pack it out" is still a good one and should be followed whenever camping in an area that has no place to dispose of waste. All the public campgrounds listed in this book provide trash receptacles. Most of the state parks and national park campgrounds have containers for both trash and recyclables. Recycle aluminum and plastic whenever possible, and encourage others to do the same. Never throw leftovers from a meal on the ground around the campsite or into the fire ring; this encourages wildlife to come into the site looking for an easy meal. Either dispose of leftovers in the trash container or store them in a secure vehicle for later disposal. Many campgrounds offer utility sinks for cleaning dishes. If sinks are provided, use them; avoid washing dishes in streams or lakes.

Take only pictures; leave only footprints. One of the reasons we camp is to be outdoors and enjoy the beauty of nature. Preserving what we find and leaving it behind allows others the same joy. Many historic structures in our parks have been tragically defaced by carving on the wood. These structures have been preserved as a look into our past; don't spoil that look for future generations. Always leave rocks, plants, and natural areas as you found them.

Build campfires sensibly. Sitting around a campfire at night is great joy for both young and old, but before lighting your fire, check with a ranger or campground host for fire regulations and conditions. If a fire ring is provided, use it. Resist the urge to build really large fires. A fire that is too big can easily get out of control. Never throw cans or glass into the fire ring; these items will not burn, and they cause an unsightly mess. Never leave a fire unattended, and whenever you leave the campsite, be sure that the fire is completely out.

Camp in harmony with wildlife. Observe wildlife from a distance. If you are camping with a pet, be sure to keep it under control. Never let your pet chase or harass wildlife. Remember: It's their home—you're just visiting.

Be a good camping neighbor. Courtesy is contagious, so spread it around. Respect other campers by holding down loud noises and voices. Quiet hours are established in most campgrounds; make yourself aware of the rules, and don't run motors or generators during quiet hours. Take only the space that is designated for your campsite; if you're not sure whether part of the site is yours or your neighbor's, be courteous and let the other site use the space. If you need the space, be considerate and ask first. Camping with your pet can be a positive experience, but keep in mind that a barking dog is a nuisance to other campers.

Following these guidelines will help in making your camping trip a more enjoyable experience for everyone. Good judgment and common sense go hand in hand with these guidelines. Remember: Practice makes habit! Camping in a socially and environmentally responsible way encourages others to follow suit—and will go a long way to ensure that future generations also have a place to camp.

Interacting with Our Environment

One reason to camp is the joy of being outdoors and experiencing nature first-hand. We all love to view wildlife up close, hike a beautiful mountain trail, or see that first wildflower bloom in spring. But along with this experience comes responsibility. Camping memories can be made more special when we take the time to enjoy nature in a positive and meaningful way. Appreciation of our natural world and the things that share this world with us is a value to be learned and shared with all who enjoy being outdoors. Those of us who fit into this category should hold an extra level of respect for the environment we share.

Wildlife

Learn to respect wildlife. Wildlife and campers often share the same territory. It's always a great experience to see a wild animal in its natural habitat, and bringing home a good memory can be made easier by following a few guidelines.

Never approach wildlife too closely. Each state or national park has a set of guidelines for how close is too close, but as a rule, if you're close enough to make an animal change its behavior, then you're probably too close. All wildlife can be dangerous if it feels threatened—no matter if it's a black bear or a chipmunk. Always give extra room to a mother animal and her young, and never back an animal into a corner—always leave an escape route for both you and the animal. **Feeding wildlife is strongly discouraged.** This can lead a wild animal to become a "panhandler" and puts both the animal and you in danger. Animals that are accustomed to being fed are more likely to be harmed by the food than helped. Human food, especially snack food, is often high in sugar, preservatives, and many other ingredients that are harmful to wild animals. In addition people are often bitten by animals they are feeding—the animal doesn't realize where the food stops and the hand begins.

In the Great Smoky Mountains and the Cherokee National Forest of East Tennessee, special consideration must be taken for camping in black bear habitat. Food storage is one of the main considerations. Food should be stored in a secure area, preferably a hard-sided camper, RV, or vehicle. Never store food or anything that smells like food in a tent. Please ask when checking in at one of the campgrounds in these areas about bears and proper food storage.

Wildflowers

Each spring visitors flock to parks and natural areas to search out spring wildflowers. The spring bloom is a highly anticipated event every year and is becoming more and more a tradition among family and friends. One tradition that needs to be broken, however, is gathering wildflowers, either to plant in a personal wildflower garden or use as a bouquet for the dining room table. It is illegal to gather or pick wildflowers in national parks. The wildflowers in our parks and sanctuaries are protected for everyone to enjoy, and when a wildflower is picked its beauty is taken from everyone else who visits that park. Many wildflowers dug up for personal gardens end up dying because they do not transplant well. Overpicking and overgathering have led to several wildflowers being protected by law as endangered.

Many of the parks in Tennessee hold annual wildflower pilgrimages where experts on the subject share their knowledge. This is a great way to interact with nature in a positive way. There are many local guidebooks on the subject of wildflowers; pick one up to take on your wildflower walks. By learning the names of wildflowers and the areas in which they grow, your knowledge and respect for them will also grow.

Trees

When camping during the heat of summer, you can really appreciate the shade provided by a large tree. It is very important when camping in a forested area not to damage the trees in the campground. A tree's bark is its skin, and damaging or breaking that skin allows disease and infection to penetrate the tree, which can lead to its death.

Never hammer nails or other sharp objects into trees. Always remove any rope or line that has been tied to a tree. Many campgrounds allow gathering firewood from the surrounding area as long as the wood is dead and downed. Never cut firewood from a live tree.

Firewood is often available from the Boy Scouts or other youth groups. Plenty of shade in a campground is always a plus, and working together we can protect our trees and ensure that future generations will have them to enjoy.

Hiking

Time spent hiking and exploring the forest can be an enjoyable part of your camping trip. Hiking is a great form of exercise and is also a way to slip a little farther back into the seclusion of the wilderness. Always check trail conditions before heading out. Most campground hosts or park rangers have updated information on trails and trail conditions.

Many hiking trails in Tennessee cover some pretty steep territory, switching back and forth as they climb steep ridgesides. Always stay on the trail; this is both for your safety and to protect the trail. Taking shortcuts at switchbacks wears a second path. Often this path is straight down, which can lead to water run-off and trail erosion. When hiking, always pack out what you carry in. It is very disconcerting to hike for some time to an out-of-the-way destination— only to find the garbage left behind by a previous hiking party.

It's Our Responsibility

Our environment, our parks and natural areas, are ours to protect and cherish. They are ours to enjoy today and preserve for future generations. As the saying goes: "Our natural lands do not belong to us; we are merely borrowing them from our children." Keeping this in mind every time you are camping and enjoying the outdoors will help ensure that your memories are positive ones.

Overview of Camping in Tennessee

There are seven agencies that oversee public campgrounds in Tennessee: the National Park Service, the USDA Forest Service, state parks, city or county parks, the Tennessee Valley Authority (TVA), and the U.S. Army Corps of Engineers. Each agency provides visitors with quality campgrounds. These agencies are listed below with a brief description of the type of campground they manage, information on what they offer, and any regulations that apply to their campgrounds.

National Park Service

The National Park Service in Tennessee manages Great Smoky Mountains National Park (GSMNP), Big South Fork National Recreation Area, and the Obey Wild and Scenic River. All three of these areas offer some type of camping. Two of the campgrounds in the Great Smoky Mountains on the Tennessee side—Elkmont and Cades Cove—accept reservations; the other three are on a first-come, first-served basis. A Golden Age Passport can be purchased at any national park by a U.S. resident age sixty-two or older. Holders of this passport receive a 50 percent discount on camping in both GSMNP and Big South Fork. Reservations are taken for both campgrounds in Big South Fork. The Obey Wild and Scenic River is primarily a kayaking and canoeing area with limited camping facilities; the Smokies and Big South Fork offer a variety of historic and recreational opportunities.

USDA Forest Service

The United States Department of Agriculture Forest Service oversees three areas that offer public camping in Tennessee: Cherokee National Forest—Northern Districts, Cherokee National Forest—Southern Districts, and Land Between the Lakes. Some of the best wild lands in the state fall under the jurisdiction of the USDA Forest Service. The campsites in these districts vary from basic with no amenities to "the works" RV camping. While there is no general admission fee to the national forests, some areas do have a small access fee.

State Parks

Tennessee's state park system is one of the best in the country, offering parks across the state in areas of unmatched natural beauty. Tennessee has forty-four state parks, and thirty-five of these offer camping facilities. There is usually a state park nearby with some sort of campground to fit any need. In 2001 Tennessee began a pilot program of charging an access fee to four of the state parks; this program should be expanded to include all state parks by 2004. Campground users will not be required to pay the $3.00-per-day access fee; instead a charge of 50 cents per person per day will be added to the daily camping fee. A few state parks are now taking reservations for campsites; I have listed the phone number for each one that does in the information on that campground. Tennessee seniors, age sixty-two and older, receive a 25 percent discount on all campsites in Tennessee state parks. You can find out more about all Tennessee state parks at www.state.tn.us/environment/parks.

City or County Parks

These are campgrounds that are either managed by a city government or under a county jurisdiction. Very few public campgrounds are run by local governments, and their amenities and conditions vary more than those of any other agency. These facilities usually are directly managed by an individual who lives on the property and handles everything from mowing the grass to collecting camping fees.

Tennessee Valley Authority (TVA)

Most Tennessee Valley Authority campgrounds are located on one of the reservoirs created by a TVA dam. They offer great lakeside camping with direct access to water activities. (TVA owns several campgrounds that are not listed in this book because they have been leased by TVA to private individuals.) Golden Age and Golden Access Passport holders receive a 50 percent discount at TVA campsites. For more information about TVA campgrounds or other river and lake information, visit www.tva.gov/river/recreation/camping.htm.

U.S. Army Corps of Engineers

All the Corps' campgrounds in Tennessee are located in Middle Tennessee. The campgrounds managed by this agency are a pleasure to visit, in most part due to the campground hosts. The campground hosts at each Corps campground are managed by an outside vendor; this creates a uniform system from campground to campground. The hosts I spoke with took great pride in their campgrounds, and it shows in the tip-top shape of their facilities. The Web site for reservations, www.ReserveUSA.com, has maps of the campgrounds along with a list of what's available.

Photography Tips

The old adage "Take only photographs, leave only footprints" is still a good philosophy for today's outdoor enthusiast. The great memories brought home from camping trips with friends and family can be made stronger or shared with others through good photographs. I have listed a few simple tips to help improve your camping trip images.

Film

Most professional photographers I know use a slower speed film (ISO 50 to 100) to capture detail for large prints. For a camping trip with the family, where you may encounter low-light conditions and be shooting subjects on the move, I suggest using a fast-speed film, one with an ISO of 200 to 400. Faster film allows a faster shutter speed, which helps eliminate blurred images when hand-holding the camera.

Steady the Camera

I always use a tripod when photographing. This ensures sharp images. Not everyone owns a tripod, and carrying one is not always convenient when on a family camping trip. Knowing how to hold the camera properly is the first step in learning how to steady the camera. With the camera to your eye, your right hand holding the camera body, and your finger on the shutter button, place the palm of your left hand under the camera body. With your palm in place, you can now use the thumb and finger of your left hand to focus the lens. Once your hands are in place, pull your elbows into your body, using your body as the brace. Placing one foot slightly in front of the other helps prevent your body from swaying and blurring the image.

You can also use another object to brace the camera. A tree, rock, vehicle, or any large object that will not move can be used to steady both you and the camera. A small beanbag or bunched up piece of clothing can be used to cradle the camera for sharper images. For example, bunch up a shirt or coat so that it creates a fluffy cushion, either on the ground or on top of something steady, preferably at eye level. Lay the camera into this "cushion" so that it is cradled but you can still see through the viewfinder.

Punching the shutter button can cause a blurry image. Instead push down on the shutter button slightly; this is all it needs to trigger the camera. One last tip on the shutter button: Anytime the camera is placed onto another object (not hand-holding) use the camera's self-timer. Most cameras have a ten-second or two-second self-timer, and using it allows the camera to stop moving after the shutter button is tripped.

Fill the Frame

The name of the game is to fill the frame. This photography philosophy might sound corny, but it carries a lot of merit. A really great photograph has impact. One way of achieving impact in an image is to fill the frame with your subject. For example: You're camping in the Great Smoky Mountains and want to take home some great photographs of the mountains in all their size and scope. Use a 100–300 mm telephoto lens. Using a wide angle to get the entire mountain range in the frame is ok, but you may find that the mountains in your images look small and not very impressive. Use the telephoto lens and fill the frame with a section of the mountains to create a stronger image.

Filling the frame also works with people. Images of your family with big scenics behind them are nice, but it's hard to see faces and expressions when people are small in the frame. Move in to show more of them and only enough background to give a sense of place.

Be careful when photographing wildlife. Frame-filling shots of animals are usually done with a very long telephoto lens by professional photographers. Don't approach too close to get that frame-filling shot. You're probably better off taking shots that show animals in their environment—it's safer for you and the animals.

Action Shots

Action shots are some of the best images from camping trips: kids swimming or at the playground, your spouse hiking on the trail or setting up camp. An image of someone doing something can have more appeal than a group shot in front of the mountains and often shows more emotion. Action photos can really bring back the way the moment felt and help keep those memories alive.

Traveling with Camera Equipment

Avoid leaving your camera in a vehicle on a hot day. The heat inside the vehicle can dry out the camera's lubrication and cause the camera to malfunction. Heat can also play havoc with film. Long exposure to heat can cause film colors to shift and therefore not render images in the way you saw them. I keep my film inside a cooler when traveling during the warmer months. If you must leave your camera in your vehicle, the trunk is cooler than in the front with all the windows.

About This Book

I have always enjoyed camping, no matter if it was on the lakeshore or on a mountain peak, but I had never put much thought into writing a book about it. Working on this book has been a wonderful experience; I have traveled back roads, been to towns I had never heard of, and talked with many new and interesting people along the way. This book is intended to be a guide to public camping in Tennessee. The campgrounds covered here are of public domain, meaning they are owned and operated by a state park, national park, city or town, or some other government organization. This isn't to say these are the only campgrounds in Tennessee. There are plenty of privately owned camping facilities, and there are many guidebooks available that cover them.

This book is broken down into three distinct sections: East Tennessee, Middle Tennessee, and West Tennessee. I've done this for two reasons: First it is to help you, the camper, find a campground in the area of Tennessee in which you want to camp. Second, this is the way everyone knows where something is in Tennessee. Ask people where they live and they will usually add what section of Tennessee they're from along with the city or town.

With each campground, I have listed the directions on how to get there. Most of the time I use a nearby town as my starting point, but sometimes I give the directions from a point or intersection of a major road or interstate. In most cases there are several ways to reach each campground; the best route really depends on where you're coming from. The signage for most campgrounds and state parks is very good, and most of my directions go with their signage. In addition to the maps and directions contained in this book, I also recommend purchasing a *DeLorme Tennessee Atlas & Gazetteer*. I found this book of detailed, large-scale maps invaluable while traveling the back roads of Tennessee.

I have included an "at a glance" chart at the beginning of each area as a quick reference to what each campground in that area has to offer. In this chart you'll find such basic information as season, number of sites, hookups, fees, and recreation offered. Because some information, like season and fees, may change from year to year, I've included a phone number for each campground that you can call for more information. Within the description of each campground, I've tried to present an idea of what you may find at each campground and additional information on what the area around the campground has to offer.

I have been told that change is inevitable, but one thing about camping has never changed: The people you meet while camping are some of the friendliest you'll ever meet. I encourage everyone to get to know your camping neighbor; you may just meet a new friend. People camp for many reasons. I have always camped just to be outdoors or to be near a place I wanted to photograph. Others camp to relax, finding that spot where it's peaceful and quiet. Some travelers camp as an inexpensive way of seeing the country, while others may be looking for recreation in their camping experience. Whatever *your* reason for camping, I hope that this book will help you find the campground that is right for you.

Campground Fee Ranges (per night)

$ = $0–$10

$$ = $11–$20

$$$ = $21–$30

$$$$ = $31 and above

LEGEND

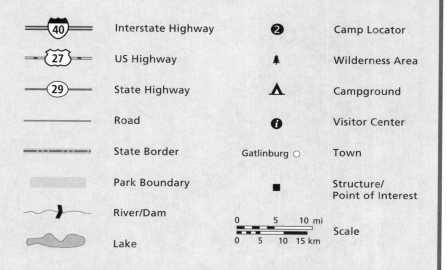

Interstate Highway	Camp Locator
US Highway	Wilderness Area
State Highway	Campground
Road	Visitor Center
State Border	Town
Park Boundary	Structure/Point of Interest
River/Dam	
Lake	Scale

Gatlinburg ○ Town

0   5   10 mi
0   5   10   15 km

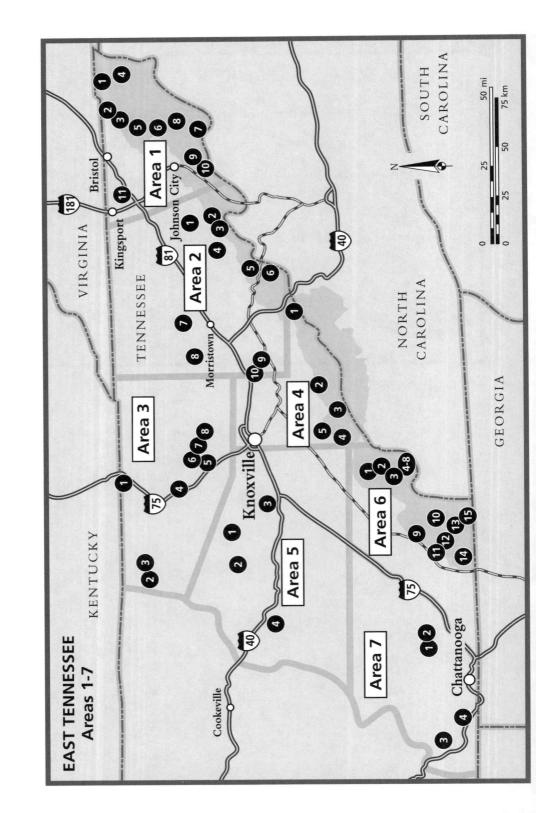

East Tennessee

Area 1
Bristol, Johnson City, and Kingsport

These cities, located in the northeast corner of Tennessee, are nicknamed "the Tri-Cities." All three are modest-size cities with a small-town feel. Here the traveler can find everything from car racing to art museums to college basketball games. Most of this area is surrounded by the Cherokee National Forest, and between the national forest and Tennessee state parks, there are more than 400 individual campsites.

For more information:

Kingsport Area Chamber of Commerce
P.O. Box 1403
151 East Main Street
Kingsport, TN 37662
(423) 392–8800
www.kingsportchamber.org

Bristol Tennessee/Virginia Chamber of Commerce
20 Volunteer Parkway
Bristol, TN 37620
(423) 989–4850
www.bristolchamber.org

1 Backbone Rock, Cherokee National Forest

Location: East of Bristol.
Sites: 11.
Facilities: Flush and vault toilets; centrally located water, fire rings, grills, tent pads, picnic tables.
Fee: $$.
Road conditions: Paved.
Management: Cherokee National Forest, Watauga Ranger District; (423) 753–1500.
Activities: Hiking, fishing, rappelling, swimming in creek allowed at your own risk. Mountain bike trails approximately 5 miles from campground in Damascus, Virginia.

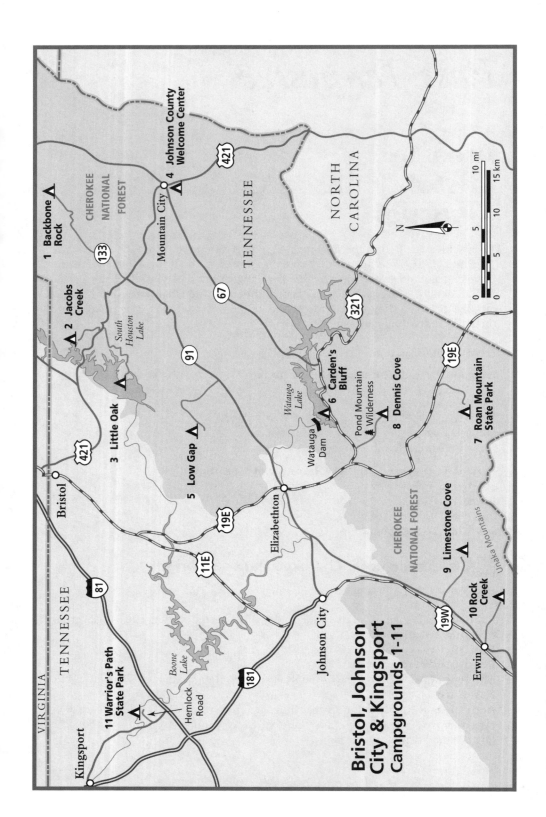

Bristol, Johnson
City & Kingsport
Campgrounds 1-11

VIRGINIA

TENNESSEE

Kingsport

Bristol

81

421

11 Warrior's Path State Park

Hemlock Road

Boone Lake

181

11E

Johnson City

19E

Elizabethton

19W

Erwin

9 Limestone Cove

Unaka Mountains

CHEROKEE
NATIONAL
FOREST

10 Rock Creek

7 Roan Mountain State Park

19E

8 Dennis Cove

Pond Mountain Wilderness

Watauga Dam

6 Carden's Bluff

Watauga Lake

321

NORTH
CAROLINA

5 Low Gap

91

3 Little Oak

2 Jacobs Creek

South Houston Lake

133

1 Backbone Rock

CHEROKEE
NATIONAL
FOREST

Mountain City

67

TENNESSEE

421

4 Johnson County Welcome Center

N

10 mi
15 km

0   5   10
0   5

	Group sites	RV sites	Total sites	Max. RV length	Hookups	Toilets	Showers	Drinking water	Dump station	Pets	Wheelchair	Recreation	Fee ($)	Season	Can reserve	Stay limit
1 Backbone Rock			11			FV	•		•	•		HSFW	$$	April–Dec.		14
2 Jacobs Creek			29			F	•	•	•	•	•	SFBLH	$$	April–Oct.		14
3 Little Oak			72			FV	•	•	•	•	•	LHFWB	$$	April–Oct.		14
4 Johnson County Welcome Center Campground	14	14		40	WES	F	•	•	•	•			$$	April–Oct.		NO LIMIT
5 Low Gap			5			V				•		HO		April–Dec.		14
6 Carden's Bluff			42			F	•	•		•		LHSFB	$	April–Oct.		14
7 Roan Mountain State Park			107			F	•	•	•	•		HSFW	$$	April–Nov.		14
8 Dennis Cove			15		E	FV	•		•			FH	$	May–Oct.		14
9 Limestone Cove			18			V	•		•			HF	$	May–Oct.		14
10 Rock Creek		11	31	35	WE	F	•	•	•	•	•	HS	$$	May–Oct.		14
11 Warrior's Path State Park			135		WE	F	•	•	•	•		FHSLBW	$$	April–Nov.		14

Hookups: W = Water E = Electric S = Sewer **Toilets:** F = Flush V = Vault P = Pit C = Chemical **Recreation:** H = Hiking S = Swimming F = Fishing B = Boating L = Boat Launch R = Horseback riding O = Off-highway driving W = Wildlife watching M = Mountain biking C = Canoeing G = Golf K = Kayaking **Maximum Trailer/RV length** given in feet. **Stay Limit** given in days. **Fee** given in dollars. If no entry under **Season**, campground is open all year. If no entry under **Fee**, camping is free.

Season: April–December.

Finding the campground: From Bristol, travel south on U.S. Highway 421 for 20 miles to Shady Valley. Turn left onto Tennessee Highway 133 for 8 miles to the recreation area. After passing through the tunnel at Backbone Rock, look for the campground entrance on the left.

The campground: Backbone Rock Campground is a small campground located adjacent to TN 133. Backbone Rock Recreation Area, named for a unique rock formation, is just south of the campground. At the turn of the twentieth century, the railroad drilled a tunnel through the ridge for logging trains to pass through. On weekends the "World's Shortest Tunnel" is a popular place for the sport of rappelling. A short trail will take the adventurous to the top of Backbone Rock. Beaverdam Creek flows through the recreation area and is stocked with trout by the Tennessee Wildlife Resources Agency (TWRA).

2   Jacobs Creek, Cherokee National Forest

Location: East of Bristol on South Holston Lake.
Sites: 29.
Facilities: Picnic tables, fire rings, and lantern posts; centrally located water and showers; flush toilets and trailer dump station. Bathhouse in Loop B meets ADA requirements.

Tunnel through Backbone Rock, Backbone Rock Recreation Area

Fee: $$.
Road conditions: Paved to gravel.
Management: Cherokee National Forest, Watauga Ranger District; (423) 735-1500.
Activities: Water sports, fishing, swimming, hiking, and shooting.
Season: April–October.
Finding the campground: From Bristol, take U.S. Highway 421 south for 12 miles, and then turn left onto paved Denton Valley Road. Travel 2 miles and turn left onto paved Jacobs Creek Road. This road becomes gravel 0.9 mile from the campground.

The campground: This campground, situated on a peninsula on South Holston Lake in the Jacobs Creek Recreation Area, is a great spot for summer water activities. The campground has a large beach area with plenty of grass for picnicking. A public boat is located about 0.5 mile west on US 421. South Holston Lake is a favorite summer destination for fishing enthusiasts, pleasure boaters, and water-skiers. The area also offers a shooting range about 1 mile from the campground. A 15-mile self-guided auto tour on Forest Road 87 provides an educational experience on how the Cherokee National Forest is managed.

3 Little Oak

Location: East of Bristol.
Sites: 72.
Facilities: Showers; flush and vault toilets; fire rings, picnic tables, lantern posts; centrally located water; dump station.
Fee: $$.
Road conditions: Paved to gravel.
Management: Cherokee National Forest, Watauga Ranger District; (423) 735-1500.
Activities: Boating, water-skiing, fishing, hiking, and wildlife watching.
Season: April–October.
Finding the campground: From Bristol, follow U.S. Highway 421 south for 12 miles and turn right onto Camp Tom Howard Road. After 0.5 mile the road becomes gravel Forest Road 87. Follow FR 87 for 6 more miles; turn right onto Forest Road 87G and follow it 1.5 miles to the campground.

The campground: Little Oak, like Jacobs Creek Campground, sits on the edge of South Holston Lake. Most campsites here have a view of Holston Lake, and several allow access to the water from the campsite. The lake offers many recreational activities, including boating, water-skiing, and fishing, but the area is also loaded with hiking opportunities. There are a couple of short trails in the recreational area and several in the surrounding areas of Holston Mountain. This area has been designated as a Watchable Wildlife Area. Early morning and late afternoon are good times to see such wildlife as white-tailed deer and wild turkeys.

4 Johnson County Welcome Center Campground

Location: Near downtown Mountain City.
Sites: 14.
Facilities: Water; sewer and electric hookups; showers, flush toilets, and dump station.
Fee: $$.
Road conditions: Paved.
Management: Johnson County Welcome Center; (423) 727-5800.
Activities: Hiking; shopping in Mountain City.
Season: April–November.
Finding the campground: The welcome center is located on U.S. Highway 421 in Mountain City; the campground is directly behind the welcome center.

The campground: This campground is better suited for RVs but does offer tent camping in an open field. The campground is located just behind the welcome center and about 3 blocks from downtown antiquing. Mountain City is a lovely small mountain town that has made a revival of its mountain history. Hiking is available in nearby Cherokee National Forest.

5 Low Gap, Cherokee National Forest

Location: North of Elizabethton.
Sites: 5.
Facilities: Picnic tables, fire rings, and lantern post; vault toilets.
Fee: No fee for camping.
Road conditions: Paved to gravel.
Management: Cherokee National Forest, Watauga Ranger District; (423) 735–1500.
Activities: Hiking.
Season: April–December.
Finding the campground: From Elizabethton take Tennessee Highway 91 north for 7 miles. Turn left onto Forest Service Road 56 and go 4 miles to fork in the road; take left fork onto Forest Service Road 202 and go 3 miles to campground.

The campground: Low Gap is a very primitive camping area with limited campsites. This is a good spot to get away from the crowds and have some peace and quiet.

6 Carden's Bluff, Cherokee National Forest

Location: North of Hampton.
Sites: 42.
Facilities: Flush toilets, showers; centrally located water; tables, grills, lantern posts.
Fee: $.
Road conditions: Paved.
Management: Cherokee National Forest, Watauga Ranger District; (423) 735–1500.
Activities: Water sports, fishing, swimming, and hiking.
Season: April–October.
Finding the campground: From Hampton take U.S. Highway 321 South/Tennessee Highway 67 East 4.1 miles to the entrance of Carden's Bluff Campground; turn left at the sign.

The campground: Overlooking 6,430-acre Watauga Lake, Carden's Bluff is a ridgetop campground with plenty of views. The campsites are at various heights on the ridge—sites at the top afford views of the lake; others are at the water's edge. There is a boat ramp 1 mile west on US 321. Hiking is available on the Carden's Bluff Trail, which starts at the campground, and also in nearby Cherokee National Forest.

7 | Roan Mountain State Park

Location: Southeast of Elizabethton.
Sites: 107.
Facilities: Tables, grills, lantern posts; centrally located water, showers; 87 sites have water and electric hookups; dump station.
Fee: $$.
Road conditions: Paved.
Management: Roan Mountain State Park; (423) 772–0190.
Activities: Hiking, swimming, and fishing.
Season: April–November; self-contained RVs November–April.
Finding the campground: Take Tennessee Highway 19E south out of Elizabethton and travel 17 miles to the town of Roan Mountain. Turn right onto Tennessee Highway 143 and go 2 miles to the park; the campground is another 2 miles past the visitor center.

The campground: Roan Mountain State Park has much to offer. It is most famous for the 600-acre natural rhododendron garden atop Roan Mountain. Peak bloom is near the end of June each year, and the park holds a Rhododendron Festival that coincides with the bloom. (Note: Camping here is first-come, first-served and the campground fills quickly during the festival.) The Appalachian Trail (AT) crosses Roan Mountain at Carver's Gap, and there are good day hiking opportunities on the AT from the campground. The park also has a swimming pool and a recreation lodge. The Doe River runs through the park, offering trout fishing in season.

8 | Dennis Cove, Cherokee National Forest

Location: East of Hampton.
Sites: 15.
Facilities: Tables, grills; electric hookups, centrally located water; flush and vault toilets.
Fee: $.
Road conditions: Paved.
Management: Cherokee National Forest, Watauga Ranger District; (423) 735–1500.
Activities: Hiking and fishing.
Season: May–October; call ranger station for updated information.
Finding the campground: From Hampton and U.S. Highway 321/Tennessee Highway 67, turn right at Citizens Bank onto Dennis Cove Road; travel 5.1 miles to the Dennis Cove Recreation Area and the campground. Caution: This is a very steep, narrow road with several switchbacks.

The campground: Dennis Cove Campground is nestled back in a secluded cove, with more of a wilderness feeling than some other campgrounds in the national forest. The campsites are located next to Laurel Creek, a small stream that is stocked with rainbow trout. Not far from the campground is Laurel

Creek Lodge, a haven for Appalachian Trail hikers. Campers from Dennis Cove can also find limited supplies and a shower at the lodge for a small price. Hiking opportunities are numerous in the Dennis Cove Recreation Area. There is no garbage pickup in the area, so you must pack out what you packed in.

9 Limestone Cove, Cherokee National Forest

Location: East of Unicoi.
Sites: 18.
Facilities: Tables, grills, lantern posts; centrally located water; vault toilets.
Fee: $.
Road conditions: Paved.
Management: Cherokee National Forest, Nolichucky/Unaka Ranger District; (423) 638-4109.
Activities: Hiking, fishing, and picnicking.
Season: May–October.
Finding the campground: From Unicoi, take Tennessee Highway 107 east 3.5 miles to Limestone Cove Recreation Area. The campground is on the right side of the highway.

The campground: This campground is smaller and more rustic but not really secluded—TN 107 passes very near some of the campsites. It is, though, a very beautiful area with large trees for shade in summer. North Indian Creek runs through the recreation area and makes a good place to cool off in the hot summer months. Trout fishing is plentiful in North Indian Creek and nearby Red Fork Creek. The Limestone Cove Trail (#30) provides hiking access to the Unaka Mountain Wilderness Area.

10 Rock Creek, Cherokee National Forest

Location: East of Erwin.
Sites: 31.
Facilities: Tables, fire rings, lantern posts, centrally located water; flush toilets and showers; stream-fed swimming pool; dump station and water hookups; 11 sites have electric hookups.
Fee: $$.
Road conditions: Paved.
Management: Cherokee National Forest, Nolichucky/Unaka Ranger District; (423) 638-4109.
Activities: Hiking, biking, and swimming.
Season: May–October.
Finding the campground: From Main Street in Erwin take Tennessee Highway 395 east for 3.5 miles to the Rock Creek Recreation Area; the entrance to the campground is on the left.

The campground: Camping here is like stepping back in time; most of the facilities were built by the Civilian Conservation Corps in the 1930s and still retain the feel of yesteryear. The USDA Forest Service constructed the campground in the 1960s. This large recreation area is a great spot to beat the summer heat. The swimming pool is fed by a small stream that forks off Rock Creek. The campground has two large double sites with electrical hookups and enough room for two large RVs. Flush toilets, showers, and water are centrally located. Several hiking trails and an easy bike trail are located in the Rock Creek Recreation Area.

11 Warrior's Path State Park

Location: East of Kingsport.
Sites: 135.
Facilities: Tables, grills; flush toilets, showers; dump station; 94 sites have water and electric hookups.
Fee: $$.
Road conditions: Paved.
Management: Warrior's Path State Park; (423) 239–7141.
Activities: Fishing, hiking, swimming, biking, boating, horseback riding, and golf.
Season: Some sites year-round.
Finding the campground: From Interstate 81 take exit 59 and travel north onto Tennessee Highway 36. Turn right onto Hemlock Road; follow signs to park entrance.

The campground: Warrior's Path is named for an ancient warpath used by the Cherokee Indians. The park sits on the shores of Fort Patrick Henry Reservoir and the Holston River, so boating, water-skiing, and fishing are among the many activities available here. The large campground is a great base for a family weekend or a short vacation. With hiking trails, Olympic-size swimming pool, horseback riding, boating, and an eighteen-hole golf course, this campground offers something for everyone in the family. Canoes, pontoon boats, and paddleboats can be rented at the marina. If you bring your own, slips can be rented to store your boat. Points to visit outside the park include Bays Mountain Nature Center and Appalachian Caverns.

Area 2
Morristown and Greeneville

Morristown and Greeneville are historic towns with lots to see and do. In Greeneville one of my favorite things to do is antiquing. Downtown has plenty of antiques shops and galleries. The Andrew Johnson National Historic Site is also in Greeneville. There you'll see some of Andrew Johnson's personal belongings and learn a lot about our seventeenth president. Morristown is an equally interesting place to visit. Here you'll find the Crockett Tavern, owned by Davy Crockett's parents and where he spent most of his boyhood. The town architecture is interesting. It's the only town I have visited that has a second-story sidewalk. Walkways above the downtown sidewalk are accessible by ramps and lead to stores that are on the "second floor."

For more information:

Morristown Area Chamber of Commerce
P.O. Box 9
Morristown, TN 37815
(423) 586–6382
www.morristownchamber.com

Greene County Partnership
115 Academy Street
Greeneville, TN 37743
(423) 638–4111
www.greenecountypartnership.com

1 Davy Crockett Birthplace State Park

Location: Northeast of Greeneville.
Sites: 74.
Facilities: Water and electric hookups; 25 sites with sewer hookups; flush toilets, dump station, showers; swimming pool; grills, tables.
Fee: $$.
Road conditions: Paved.
Management: Davy Crockett Birthplace State Park; (423) 257–2167.
Activities: Swimming, fishing, boating.
Season: Campground is open year-round.
Finding the campground: From Greeneville take U.S. Highway 11E north for approximately 10 miles. Turn right onto South Heritage Rd (Old Route 34); go 1.2 miles and turn right onto Davy Crockett Road. Travel another 1.2 miles and Davy Crockett Road takes a sharp right curve and joins Keebler Road. From here it is 0.9 mile to the entrance to Davy Crockett Birthplace State Park.

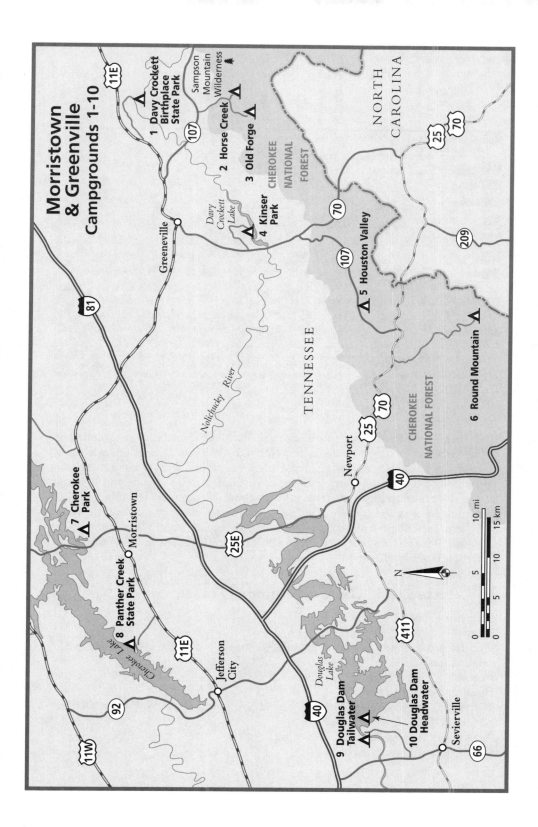

Morristown & Greenville Campgrounds 1-10

1 Davy Crockett Birthplace State Park

Sampson Mountain Wilderness

2 Horse Creek

3 Old Forge

107

CHEROKEE NATIONAL FOREST

4 Kinser Park

Davy Crockett Lake

Greeneville

81

Nolichucky River

TENNESSEE

NORTH CAROLINA

25

70

209

70

107

5 Houston Valley

6 Round Mountain

CHEROKEE NATIONAL FOREST

25

70

Newport

40

411

66

Sevierville

Douglas Lake

9 Douglas Dam Tailwater

10 Douglas Dam Headwater

40

11E

Jefferson City

8 Panther Creek State Park

Cherokee Lake

92

11W

7 Cherokee Park

Morristown

25E

11E

	Group sites	RV sites	Total sites	Max. RV length	Hookups	Toilets	Showers	Drinking water	Dump station	Pets	Wheelchair	Recreation	Fee ($)	Season	Can reserve	Stay limit
1 Davy Crockett Birthplace State Park	•	35	74	45	EWS	F	•	•	•	•	•	SHFB	$$			NO LIMIT
2 Horse Creek		2	15	60		FV	•		•	•		HFSO	$	April–Dec.		14
3 Old Forge			10			V	•		•	•		HRFOS	$	April–Dec.		14
4 Kinser Park	•	157	157	45	EWS	F	•	•		•		HSFLB	$$	April–Nov.		14
5 Houston Valley	•	7	8	20		F	•		•			H	$	April–Dec.		14
6 Round Mountain		2	14	35		V	•		•			HW	$	April–Dec.		14
7 Cherokee Park		52	65	35	EW	F	•	•	•	•	•	FLBH	$$	March–Oct.		14
8 Panther Creek State Park		50	50	NO MAX	EW	F	•	•	•	•	•	LFHW	$$	March–Nov.		14
9 Douglas Dam Tailwater		64	64	60	EW	F	•	•	•	•	•	LFB	$$	March–Nov.		21
10 Douglas Dam Headwater		61	65	40	EW	F	•	•	•	•	•	FLBSH	$$	March–Nov.		30

Hookups: W = Water E = Electric S = Sewer **Toilets:** F = Flush V = Vault P = Pit C = Chemical **Recreation:** H = Hiking S = Swimming F = Fishing B = Boating L = Boat Launch R = Horseback riding O = Off-highway driving W = Wildlife watching M = Mountain biking C = Canoeing G = Golf K = Kayaking **Maximum Trailer/RV length** given in feet. **Stay Limit** given in days. **Fee** given in dollars. If no entry under **Season,** campground is open all year. If no entry under **Fee,** camping is free.

The campground: The campground here has a very basic layout—situated on a flat piece of land not far from the Nolichucky River. It is open, with only part of the campground having large trees for shade. The campground sites could be improved by adding grills and fire rings. Some sites are on the banks of the river, and there is river access for anyone wishing to fish. The interesting thing here is the history. The park and its facilities pay tribute to Davy Crockett, legendary frontier hero. The park's museum tells the story of his life, and there is a replica of the log cabin where Davy was born on the banks of the Nolichucky River.

2 Horse Creek, Cherokee National Forest

Location: East of Greeneville.
Sites: 15.
Facilities: Flush and vault toilets; tables, fire rings, lantern posts; centrally located water.
Fee: $.
Road conditions: Paved.
Management: Cherokee National Forest, Nolichucky/Unaka Ranger District; (423) 638–4109.
Activities: Hiking, fishing, swimming.
Season: April–December.

Paved walkway to swimming and picnic area at Horse Creek

Finding the campground: From Tusculum in Greeneville take Tennessee Highway 107 north 6.5 miles. Turn right onto Horse Creek Road and go 2.5 miles to the campground entrance.

The campground: This is a beautiful campground located just inside the Cherokee National Forest and the foothills of the Appalachian Mountains. Large hemlock trees shade most of the campground, and Horse Creek flows through the middle of the area. At the time of my visit, floods had damaged the campground, but efforts were under way to clean up and rebuild some of the damaged areas. From May 15 to October 15 only disabled persons, children under the age of twelve, and seniors are allowed to fish in the section of Horse Creek that runs through the recreation area. There are several hiking trail in the nearby Sampson Mountain Wilderness.

3 Old Forge, Cherokee National Forest

Location: East of Greeneville.
Sites: 10.
Facilities: Vault toilets; centrally located water pump; fire rings, tables, lantern posts. There is a horse corral next to the camping area.
Fee: $.
Road conditions: Dirt road, rough.
Management: Cherokee National Forest, Nolichucky/Unaka Ranger District; (423) 638-4109.
Activities: Horseback riding, hiking, fishing, swimming.
Season: April–December.
Finding the campground: From Tusculum in Greeneville take Tennessee Highway 107 north 6.5 miles. Turn right onto Horse Creek Road and go 2.5 miles to the entrance to Horse Creek Recreation Area. Turn right onto Forest Road 331 (Old Forge Road), and travel 2.7 miles to the campground.

The campground: Old Forge is a secluded, quiet area to camp. Located at the dead end of FR 331, it's a peaceful place to spend a weekend. The entire campground has walk-in sites only, but they are a short distance from the parking area. Each site is very well marked off, with each site having a large area to pitch a tent. All sites are wheelchair-accessible, but the rest rooms do not meet ADA requirements. Old Forge is a great destination for the equestrian, having more than 8 miles of horse trails. Jennings Creek, which flows along the edge of the campground, is a good place to fish, wade, swim, or relax.

4 Kinser Park

Location: South of Greeneville.
Sites: 157.
Facilities: Tables, grills; golf course, waterslide, minigolf, volleyball; flush toilets; water, electric, and sewer hookups.
Fee: $$.

Scenic overlook at Jennings Creek, Old Forge Campground

Road conditions: Paved.
Management: The City of Greeneville and Greene County; (423) 639–5912.
Reservations: (423) 639–5912.
Activities: Boating, golf (nine-hole course), minigolf, volleyball, baseball, waterslide, fishing.
Season: April–November.
Finding the campground: From Greeneville take Tennessee Highway 70 south 6.2 miles and turn left onto East Allens Bridge Road. Go 2.5 miles and turn right onto Canary Road; go 0.1 mile to a stop sign. At the stop sign turn right and go 0.9 mile, and then turn right onto Kinser Park Lane. From here it is 0.7 mile to the park entrance.

The campground: This is an excellent park for the family. Its recreation facilities are almost too numerous to list. Besides being a very clean and well-organized campground, Kinser also offers a nine-hole golf course, a minigolf course, baseball and softball fields, a waterslide, a volleyball court, and a basketball court. If that's not enough, Kinser Park is located on the banks of the Nolichucky River, offering boating and fishing opportunities.

5 | Houston Valley, Cherokee National Forest

Location: South of Greeneville.
Sites: 8.
Facilities: Tables, fire rings, lantern posts. The campground and picnic area share two flush toilets.
Fee: $.
Road conditions: Paved road to campground; gravel in campground.
Management: Cherokee National Forest, Nolichucky/Unaka Ranger District; (423) 638–4109.
Activities: Hiking, relaxing, picnicking; nearby rifle range.
Season: April–December.
Finding the campground: From Greeneville take Tennessee Highway 70 south 10 miles. Turn right onto Tennessee Highway 107 west and go 9 miles; Houston Valley campground is on the left.

The campground: Houston Valley is a small campground and picnic area, located just a few yards off TN 107. While this is more of a primitive campground with unimproved sites, the sites are spaced out with plenty of room between them. Most of the sites are on a slight hillside. Forest Service information indicates that seven of the sites can accommodate 20-foot trailers. I didn't measure the pull-in sites, but they look smaller than that to me. The Weaver Bend Watchable Wildlife Area is located nearby, as well as many hiking trails.

6 | Round Mountain, Cherokee National Forest

Location: South of Greeneville.
Sites: 14.
Facilities: Tables, fire rings, lantern posts; centrally located water; vault toilets.
Fee: $.
Road conditions: Gravel, very narrow and winding.
Management: Cherokee National Forest, Nolichucky/Unaka Ranger District; (423) 638–4109.
Activities: Hiking, relaxing, and wildflower viewing in spring.
Season: April–December.
Finding the campground: From Greeneville take Tennessee Highway 70 south 10 miles. Turn right onto Tennessee Highway 107: travel 13 miles. Turn right onto U.S. Highway 25/70 and go 3 miles; turn left on TN 107. From here follow signs to the campground.

The campground: This is a very remote, secluded campground. If your idea of camping is getting away to a more quiet area, this would be a good choice. With an elevation of approximately 3,100 feet, it is also one of the cooler areas in summer. The two most popular things to do here are hiking and wildflower viewing. There are several locations for the hiker to access the Appalachian Trail, and Max Patch—a popular destination for seeing wildflowers—is near here.

7 Cherokee Park

Location: Morristown.
Sites: 65.
Facilities: Showers, flush toilets, dump station; electric and water hookups; children's wading pool, two playgrounds, volleyball courts; pavilions and shelters.
Fee: $$.
Road conditions: Paved.
Management: Hamblen County; (423) 586-0325.
Activities: Fishing, picnicking, volleyball, children's playground.
Season: March–October.
Finding the campground: From Morristown take U.S. Highway 25E; go 2.3 miles and turn right onto Cherokee Park Road. Go 0.2 mile; the entrance to Cherokee Park is on the left.

The campground: Cherokee Park is a county park of which the campground is a part. With rolling hills and fields to walk in, this is a good setting for a family outing. From talking with the staff of the campground, it is evident that this is a family-oriented park. The campground itself is located on the shore of Cherokee Lake, which is well known for its fishing. The campground is well shaded by large trees, mostly oaks, with large spaces to spread out the camping gear. A nearby boat dock provides boat launching, rental boats, and concessions.

Hamblen County Marina, next to Cherokee Park Campground

8 Panther Creek State Park

Location: South of Morristown.
Sites: 50.
Facilities: Tables, grills, lantern posts, fire rings; electric and water hookups; showers, flush toilets; swimming pool; dump station and laundromat.
Fee: $$.
Road conditions: Paved.
Management: Panther Creek State Park; (423) 587–7046.
Activities: Hiking, boating, fishing, horseback riding (must bring own horse), swimming, volleyball, tennis, horseshoes, playgrounds.
Season: March–November; some camping available year-round with no water.
Finding the campground: From Morristown take U.S. Highway 11E south to Tennessee Highway 342W. Turn right onto TN 342W and travel 2.3 miles to the entrance to Panther Creek State Park.

The campground: When I visited this campground it was very well manicured and clean. It seemed to be well suited for RVs and tents. The campground is very open from site to site, giving it almost a commercial campground feel. There are several great spots around the park; not far from the campground is a great picnic area that is well shaded and a good spot for an afternoon lunch. Watching the sunset over Cherokee Lake from Point Lookout, the highest point in the park at 1,460 feet, is a popular evening pastime.

9 Douglas Dam Tailwater

Location: North of Sevierville.
Sites: 64.
Facilities: Showers, flush toilets; tables, fire rings; boat launch, playground; electric and water hookups at some sites.
Fee: $$.
Road conditions: Paved.
Management: Tennessee Valley Authority; (866) 494–7186.
Activities: Boating, fishing, relaxing.
Season: March–November.
Finding the campground: From Tennessee Highway 66 in Sevierville, take Tennessee Highway 338 north for 6 miles; entrance to the campground is on the right.

The campground: Fishing seems to be the big draw to this campground on the banks of the French Broad River. There are sixty-four sites here divided into two sections by the road that runs through the campground. One section is on the banks of the river; the other section is across the road. A stay limit of twenty-one days is strictly enforced on the riverside, but after the twenty-one days you can move your camp to the other section. This campground and the Douglas Dam Headwater Campground could be good places to stay if you are visiting one of the tourist towns of Pigeon Forge or Sevierville.

Campsite on the shore of Douglas Lake, Douglas Dam Headwater

10 Douglas Dam Headwater

Location: North of Sevierville.
Sites: 65.
Facilities: Showers, flush toilets, dump station; centrally located water; tables, grills; boat launch, beach area.
Fee: $$.
Road conditions: Paved.
Management: Tennessee Valley Authority; (866) 494–7186.
Activities: Fishing, boating, water-skiing, swimming, nature trails.
Season: March–November.
Finding the campground: From Tennessee Highway 66 in Sevierville, take Tennessee Highway 338 north for 4.2 miles. Turn right onto Boat Launch Road and go 1 mile; campground entrance is on the right.

The campground: Douglas Dam Headwater is above the dam, as we would say, meaning that it is next to the lake created by the dam. Here you will find plenty of open water for just about any water activity you can think of. Some campsites are on the shore, and some are on a hill overlooking the lake. Boats can be moored at several of the lakeside sites. According to the TVA office, the stay limit here is thirty days, but some sites are available for long-term rental.

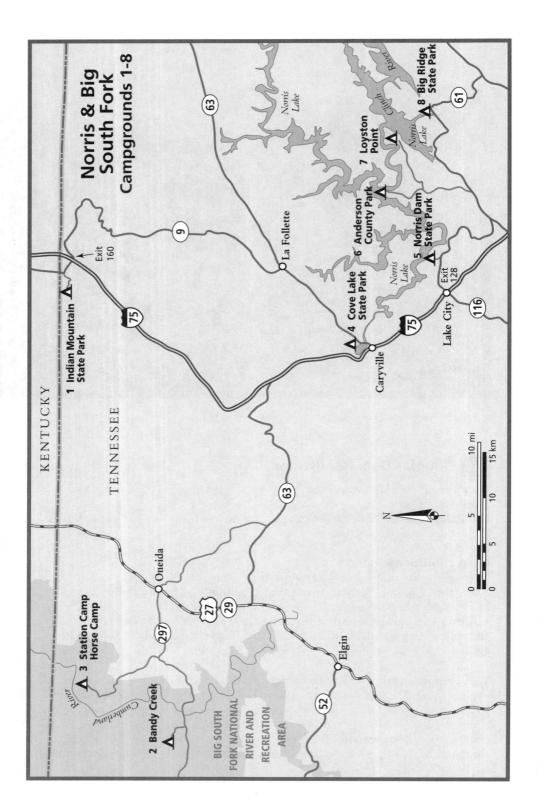

Norris & Big South Fork Campgrounds 1-8

KENTUCKY

TENNESSEE

1 Indian Mountain State Park

Exit 160

75

9

63

3 Station Camp Horse Camp

Cumberland River

2 Bandy Creek

297

Oneida

27

29

BIG SOUTH FORK NATIONAL RIVER AND RECREATION AREA

63

Elgin

52

La Follette

Norris Lake

7 Loyston Point

Clinch River

8 Big Ridge State Park

61

6 Anderson County Park

5 Norris Dam State Park

Norris Lake

4 Cove Lake State Park

Caryville

Norris Lake

75

Lake City

Exit 128

116

N

0   5   10 mi
0   5   10   15 km

Area 3
Norris and Big South Fork

Norris, Tennessee, started out as a planned community for the workers constructing Norris Dam. The original town plan was adopted from England's garden city movement of the 1890s—the buildings and houses were built on smaller lots with large open areas known as commons. The original houses were built from twelve basic designs, and today you can still see many of these first buildings. The town has grown but has maintained its roots as a family-friendly community.

The Big South Fork National River and Recreation Area was set aside to protect this section of the Cumberland Plateau's natural beauty and to provide economic growth from recreation instead of coal mining and timber cutting. The area is maintained by the National Park Service and provides such outdoor activities as kayaking, canoeing, rafting, hiking, mountain biking, horseback riding, hunting, and fishing. The 110,000-acre recreation area is shared by Tennessee and Kentucky.

For more information:

Big South Fork National River and Recreation Area
(Bandy Creek Visitor Center)
4564 Leatherwood Road
Oneida, TN 37841
(423) 286–7275
www.nps.gov/biso

Anderson County Chamber of Commerce
245 North Main Street, Suite 200
Clinton, TN 37716
(865) 457–2559
www.andersoncountychamber.org

	Group sites	RV sites	Total sites	Max. RV length	Hookups	Toilets	Showers	Drinking water	Dump station	Pets	Wheelchair	Recreation	Fee ($)	Season	Can reserve	Stay limit
1 Indian Mountain State Park		49	49	45	WE	F	•	•	•	•		FBWS	$$	April–Nov.		14
2 Bandy Creek	•	97	146	65	WE	F	•	•	•	•	•	SHRMK	$$		•	14
3 Station Camp Horse Camp		24	24	45	WE	F	•	•		•		HRK	$$–$$$$	Mar.–Nov.	•	NO LIMIT
4 Cove Lake State Park		97	97	50	WE	F	•	•	•	•		BWFS	$$	May–Nov.		14
5 Norris Dam State Park	•	25	85	NO MAX	WE	F	•	•	•	•	•	HFBSL	$$	April–Oct.		14
6 Anderson County Park	•	26	57	40	WE	F	•	•	•	•		FSBHL	$$	April–Oct.		21
7 Loyston Point		39	63	45	E	F	•	•	•	•	•	HSFBL	$$	Mar.–Oct.		21
8 Big Ridge State Park		3	50	45	WE	F	•	•	•	•	•	HSF	$$	April–Nov.		14

Hookups: W = Water E = Electric S = Sewer **Toilets:** F = Flush V = Vault P = Pit C = Chemical **Recreation:** H = Hiking S = Swimming F = Fishing B = Boating L = Boat Launch R = Horseback riding O = Off-highway driving W = Wildlife watching M = Mountain biking C = Canoeing G = Golf K = Kayaking **Maximum Trailer/RV length** given in feet. **Stay Limit** given in days. **Fee** given in dollars. If no entry under **Season**, campground is open all year. If no entry under **Fee**, camping is free.

1 Indian Mountain State Park

Location: Near the town of Jellico.
Sites: 49.
Facilities: Tables, grills, fire rings; showers, flush toilets, dump station; swimming pool; electric and water hookups.
Fee: $$.
Road conditions: Paved.
Management: Indian Mountain State Park; (423) 784–7958.
Activities: Swimming, fishing, pedal boats, wildlife watching, walking.
Season: April–November. Camping is allowed year-round, but all water is shut off around November 1.
Finding the campground: From Interstate 75 in Jellico, take exit 160 and go north on U.S. Highway 25 to Tennessee Highway 297. Make a right onto London Street and a left onto Dairy Street to the park entrance; watch for park signs.

The campground: This is a very well kept campground not far from Jellico, Tennessee, and the Kentucky state line. The unique feature here is that this campground and state park is developed on a reclaimed strip mine. This is one of the best reclaiming projects that I have seen done on old mining property. The park has two small lakes or ponds for fishing; pedal boats are available to rent. While there is not a lot of hiking to be done here, the park does have two walking trails—one paved, the other unpaved. This park is also a good place for wildlife watching, which is best in the early morning and late afternoon hours.

2 Bandy Creek, Big South Fork National River and Recreation Area

Location: West of Oneida.

Sites: 146.

Facilities: Tables, fire rings, lantern poles; electric and water hookups; showers, flush toilets, dump station; horse stables, swimming pool.

Fee: $$.

Road conditions: Paved.

Management: Big South Fork National River and Recreation Area, National Park Service; (423) 286–8368.

Reservations: (800) 365–2267, Code: 244 (Big); www.reservations.nps.gov.

Activities: Hiking, horseback riding, mountain biking, swimming, canoeing and kayaking, fishing.

Season: Year-round.

Finding the campground: From Oneida take Tennessee Highway 297 west for 5 miles. TN 297 bears left and becomes TN 297–Leatherwood Ford Road. Continue for 7.2 miles; the entrance road is on the right. Watch for signs. (Caution: Parts of this road are very steep and curvy.)

Horse stables near Bandy Creek Campground, Big South Fork National River and Recreation Area

The campground: This is one of the best campgrounds I have visited. It's very clean and well kept, and the sites are nicely spaced with plenty of room. Most sites are shaded. Big South Fork has two major draws, horseback riding and kayaking. There are stables very near the campground for those wishing to board their horses while camping at Bandy Creek. The stables offer easy access to the area's extensive trail system. Big South Fork has long been known for exciting white-water canoeing and kayaking. The area has several streams with varying degrees of difficulty, from beginner to very advanced white water. Fishing is also a popular activity here.

3 Station Camp Horse Camp, Big South Fork National River and Recreation Area

Location: West of Oneida.
Sites: 24.
Facilities: Tables, lantern poles, showers, grills; flush toilets; water and electric hookups; tie-outs for four horses per site.
Fee: $$–$$$$; fee is set on number of horses at each camp.
Road conditions: Paved; gravel in campground.
Management: Big South Fork National River and Recreation Area, National Park Service; (423) 569–3321.
Reservations: (423) 569–3321.
Activities: Horseback riding, kayaking and canoeing, hiking.
Season: March–November.
Finding the campground: From Oneida take Tennessee Highway 297 west 5 miles. Turn right onto Station Camp Road and go 4.1 miles; campground entrance is on the right.

The campground: This campground was planned and built with the true horse lover in mind. Your horse can be tied out right next to your campsite. The tie-outs are well planned, with a tray to hold horse feed at head level. A concrete slab where the horse stands makes cleanup easier. The sites are large, with enough room for very large horse trailers.

4 Cove Lake State Park

Location: Caryville.
Sites: 97.
Facilities: Water and electric hookups; showers, flush toilets, dump station; grills, tables; park restaurant.
Fee: $$.
Road conditions: Paved.
Management: Cove Lake State Park; (423) 566–9701.
Activities: Swimming, playground, paddleboats, biking, tennis, fishing, volleyball, hiking, wildlife watching.
Season: May–November.

Campers preparing dinner at Station Camp Horse Camp, Big South Fork National River and Recreation Area

Finding the campground: Cove Lake State Park is located in the city limits of Caryville. From Interstate 75 take exit 134 to U.S. Highway 25W in Caryville. The entrance to the park is 0.8 mile from I–75.

The campground: This is a wonderful camping facility; some sites are on Cove Lake, some are in shady areas, and there are a few open campsites. The campground offers clean shower houses and rest rooms. On my visit the campgrounds had a very clean and well-maintained appearance. There is good fishing and wildlife viewing at 210-acre Cove Lake. The paved walking and biking trail is a good place to stretch your legs. The park has an Olympic-sized swimming pool and also a kiddie pool, with lifeguards on duty.

5   Norris Dam State Park

Location: Northeast of Lake City.
Sites: 85 in two camping areas.
Facilities: Tables, grills, lantern poles; centrally located water; showers, flush toilets, dump station; swimming pool, marina, playgrounds.
Fee: $$.
Road conditions: Paved.
Management: Norris Dam State Park; (865) 426–7461.

Fishing from wildlife viewing tower, Cove Lake State Park

Activities: Swimming, hiking, boating and water-skiing, fishing.
Season: April–October; some sites open year-round.
Finding the campground: From Interstate 75 near Lake City, take exit 128 onto U.S. Highway 441; follow signs 3 miles to park entrance.

The campground: Norris Dam State Park's campgrounds are divided into two areas, an east campground and a west campground. The east campground is mostly tent sites with some hookups, as well as a primitive camping area. All sites in the west campground have electrical and water hookups. I would recommend either area, as both are very good. The park abuts Norris Lake and has great fishing, boating, and water sport activities. Norris Dam was one of the first dams built by the Tennessee Valley Authority. But this is not the only history here. Your visit should include a stop at the eighteenth-century gristmill, the historic threshing barn, and the W. G. Lenoir Pioneer Museum.

6 Anderson County Park

Location: Andersonville.
Sites: 57.
Facilities: Tables, grills; electrical and water hookups; flush toilets, dump station, showers.
Fee: $$.
Road conditions: Paved.
Management: Anderson County, park office; (865) 494-9352.
Activities: Boating and fishing, water-skiing, swimming, walking trails, playground.
Season: April–October.
Finding the campground: From Interstate 75 take exit 122 at Norris onto Tennessee Highway 61 east. Go 3.8 miles and turn left onto Park Lane; stay on Park Lane 7.3 miles into Anderson County Park.

The campground: This really nice park is run by the local government of Anderson County. Even though this is already a good campground, improvements are being made. The campground is located on Norris Lake, and several sites allow you to have your boat moored right at the campsite. There is a boat launch very near the campground and also a beach area and playground, with a very large grassy area for sunbathing. There is a twenty-one-day camping limit, but site rental by the month is available. There are 2.5 miles of hiking trails around the camping area and some very neat rock formations to explore.

7 Loyston Point

Location: North of the town of Norris.
Sites: 63.
Facilities: Showers, flush toilets, dump station; boat launch, beach; tables, grills, fire rings, tent pads and lantern posts; electrical hookups; centrally located water.
Fee: $$.

Road conditions: Paved.
Management: Tennessee Valley Authority; (865) 632–1606 or (865) 494–9399.
Activities: Boating and fishing, water-skiing and water sports, swimming.
Season: March–October.
Finding the campground: From Interstate 75 take exit 122 at Norris onto Tennessee Highway 61 east. Go 3.8 miles and turn left onto Park Lane; go 3.7 miles and turn right onto Forgety Road. Go 0.6 mile; Forgety Road ends at Mill Creek Road. Turn left onto Mill Creek Road and go 0.8 mile; turn right onto a road with no road sign. Go 0.1 mile and turn left onto Loyston Point Road. Here will be a sign for the campground; follow this road 2.8 miles to the campground entrance.

The campground: Loyston Point is located on Norris Lake. The campground has several sites next to the water; all sites are within walking distance of the lake. Boats can be moored at the lakeside campsites. This seems to be a popular destination for locals on the weekend, with the swimming beach being a big draw. There is a nearby boat ramp with lots of parking available. The sites not on the water enjoy views of the lake, and several are very shaded. This is a good location for any kind of water activity.

RVs at Norris Lake, Big Ridge State Park

8 Big Ridge State Park

Location: Northeast of Norris.
Sites: 50.
Facilities: Tables, grills; beach, playground; showers, flush toilets, dump station; water and electrical hookups.
Fee: $$.
Road conditions: Paved.
Management: Big Ridge State Park; (865) 992-5523.
Activities: Fishing, swimming, playground, hiking, tennis, ball fields, boating.
Season: April–November; some sites are open year-round, but the bathhouse is closed.
Finding the campground: From Interstate 75 near Norris take exit 122 and go east on Tennessee Highway 61 for 11.9 miles. Turn left on Big Ridge Road; this is the entrance to the park.

The campground: Part of this park's campground is on Norris Lake, but very few sites are actually on the water—and they fill early. On the other side of the park is Cove Lake; it is dammed off Norris Lake, forming a private lake for Big Ridge State Park. No private boats are allowed here, but canoes, rowboats and paddleboats rentals are available.

Area 4
Great Smoky Mountains National Park

The Smokies, as they are known by locals and lovers of the park, comprise the country's most visited national park. It is within one day's drive of more than half the nation's population. However, this is not the only reason the Smokies are so popular. With more than a half-million acres of natural beauty, the Smokies can boast several impressive facts. The park is an International Biosphere Reserve, has more tree species than all Northern Europe, counts for half the old-growth forest in the United States, and contains more wildflower species than any other national park in the country.

If you enjoy hiking, the park has more than 800 miles of trails, including trails for horseback riding and part of the Appalachian Trail. The park is home to miles and miles of clear mountain streams, great for both trout fishing and swimming on a hot summer day. Wildlife watching is also a great pastime here. White-tailed deer and black bears are two of the favorite animals to be seen in the park, but many more make the Smokies their home. Cades Cove is the most popular place for wildlife watching but is also a great area for bicycle riding, horseback riding, auto touring, learning about history, or just relaxing. There is no admission fee to this national park, so come on in and enjoy the mountains.

For more information:

Great Smoky Mountains National Park
107 Park Headquarters Road
Gatlinburg, TN 37738
(865) 436–1200
www.nps.gov/grsm

1 Cosby

Location: The northern tip of the park.
Sites: 157.
Facilities: Tables, grills, fire rings, lantern posts, tent pads; flush toilets, dump station; centrally located drinking water.
Fee: $$.
Road conditions: Paved.
Management: Great Smoky Mountains National Park; (423) 436–1230.
Activities: Hiking, fishing, wildlife watching.
Season: May–October.

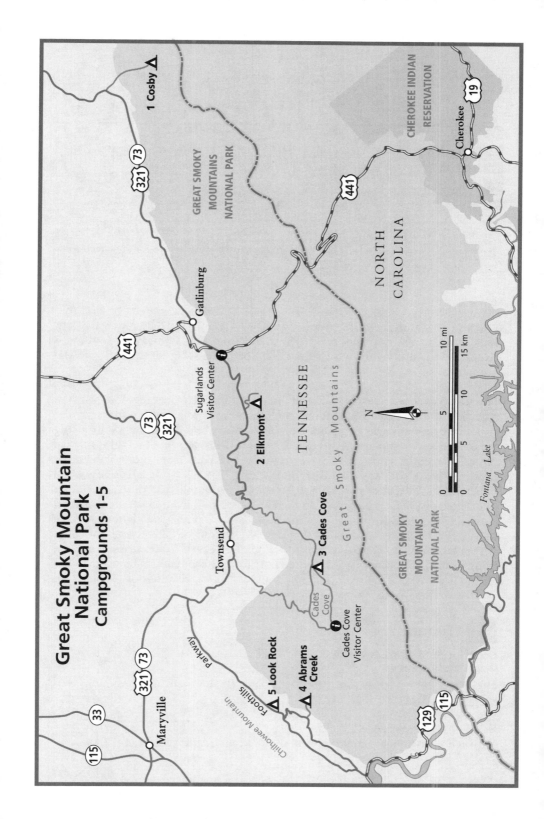

	Group sites	RV sites	Total sites	Max. RV length	Hookups	Toilets	Showers	Drinking water	Dump station	Pets	Wheelchair	Recreation	Fee ($)	Season	Can reserve	Stay limit
1 Cosby	•		157	25		F		•	•	•	•	HWF	$$	May–Oct.		7
2 Elkmont	•	197	220	34		F		•	•	•	•	HSWF	$$	May–Oct.	•	7
3 Cades Cove	•	139	161	40		F		•	•	•	•	HWRM	$$		•	7
4 Abrams Creek			18	21		F		•		•		SFH	$$	May–Oct.		14
5 Look Rock, Foothills Parkway	•	62	62	30		F		•	•	•	•	H	$$	May–Oct.		14

Hookups: W = Water E = Electric S = Sewer **Toilets:** F = Flush V = Vault P = Pit C = Chemical **Recreation:** H = Hiking S = Swimming F = Fishing B = Boating L = Boat Launch R = Horseback riding O = Off-highway driving W = Wildlife watching M= Mountain biking C = Canoeing G = Golf K = Kayaking **Maximum Trailer/RV length** given in feet. **Stay Limit** given in days. **Fee** given in dollars. If no entry under **Season**, campground is open all year. If no entry under **Fee**, camping is free.

Finding the campground: From Gatlinburg take U.S. Highway 321 North 18.2 miles. At the stop sign turn right onto Tennessee Highway 32 south and go 1.2 miles; turn right onto Cosby Park Road and follow it 2.1 miles to the campground.

The campground: Cosby is one of the more primitive campgrounds in the park. It is a little more remote than the others, so it gets fewer visitors. At the time I visited, work was being done on the campground; bathrooms were being remodeled and tent pads were being replaced. Cosby is sort of on a hillside, so several sites have steps up to or down to the tent pads from the parking area. However, some sites are level with the parking. The two wheelchair-accessible sites are very nice, some of the best I have seen in public camping. This is not a campground for large motor homes. The paved pull-in sites are smaller than most, and the road through the campground is small with some tight turns. The campground host recommended that any RVs should be 25 feet and under.

A main draw at Cosby is the hiking trails. Several trails leave from the campground, and several more branch off from those. One trails leads to the Mount Cramer Fire Tower, a very popular hiking destination. Fishing in nearby streams is also a popular activity.

2 Elkmont

Location: Off Little River Road.
Sites: 220.
Facilities: Tables, grills, fire rings, tent pads; flush toilets, dump station; centrally located water.
Fee: $$.
Road conditions: Paved.
Management: Great Smoky Mountains National Park; (423) 436–1230.

Relaxing streamside at Elkmont Campground, Great Smoky Mountains National Park

Reservations: (800) 365–2267.
Activities: Hiking, fishing, wildlife watching, swimming.
Season: May–October.
Finding the campground: From Gatlinburg take U.S. Highway 441 2 miles to the Sugarlands Visitor Center and turn right onto Little River Road. Go 4.9 miles and turn left into Elkmont at sign. Follow this road 1.5 miles to the campground.

The campground: Elkmont was once a small community before the park bought the land. There are still several reminders of that community, including the old hotel and several vacation cottages, which are no longer used. This is a great campground, very large with three different camping sections. A stream that runs through the campground is used by both fishing enthusiasts and swimmers looking to beat the summer heat. The campground is well maintained, with large sites. The official word is that the campground can handle RVs of 34-foot length, but I saw several that were much larger. Elkmont is a good central location for visiting both the Gatlinburg and Townsend areas.

3   Cades Cove

Location: South end of the park near Townsend.
Sites: 161.
Facilities: Tables, lantern posts, fire rings, grills; flush toilets, dump station; centrally located water; camp store and riding stables.
Fee: $$.
Road conditions: Paved.
Management: Great Smoky Mountains National Park; (865) 436–1230; campground number (865) 448–2472.
Reservations: (800) 365–2267.
Activities: Hiking, bicycling, horseback riding, wildlife watching, auto touring.
Season: Year-round; no reservations taken between November 1 and May 14.
Finding the campground: From Townsend take U.S. Highway 321 north 1.2 miles to Little River Road. Turn right onto Laurel Creek Road and go 7.5 miles into Cades Cove; turn left at the sign and go 0.2 mile to campground.

The campground: This is one of the more popular camping spots in the park, due in part to the fact that Cades Cove is a very well known area for wildlife watching. There is also great historical significance in this valley. A one-way, 11-mile loop road travels around the cove and returns near the campground. There are many stops along the way to view old homesteads and rustic cabins. During early morning and late afternoon, you can see white-tailed deer and sometimes black bears in the fields along the road. The campground is a nice one, with plenty of shade and large, level spots. It is very common for the wildlife to roam through the campground, so food storage regulations are strictly enforced. A riding stable near the campground provides visitors an opportunity to rent horses and ride the trails around the cove.

4   Abrams Creek

Location: Near Fontana Lake.
Sites: 18.
Facilities: Tables, fire rings, grills, lantern posts; flush toilets; centrally located water.
Fee: $$.
Road conditions: Paved, steep and narrow.
Management: Great Smoky Mountains National Park; (865) 436–1230.
Activities: Hiking, swimming, fishing.
Season: May–October.
Finding the campground: From Maryville take U.S. Highway 321 north 10 miles to the Foothills Parkway. Turn right onto the parkway and go west 16.9 miles to where the parkway ends at U.S. Highway 129. Turn left and go 0.1 mile; turn left onto Happy Valley Road and travel 6 miles. Look for the Abrams Creek Campground sign, and turn right onto Abrams Creek Road; follow this road 0.7 mile to the campground. (Caution: The road into the campground is very steep and narrow in places, with room for only one vehicle.)

Mountain stream in the Smokies

The campground: Abrams Creek is very secluded and used mostly by locals and people looking to get away from the crowds. It is a smaller camping area, and the eighteen sites fill quickly on summer weekends. There are hiking trails near the campground. Abrams Creek flows through the campground, providing swimming and fishing opportunities. During summer it's a great place to stay cool because of the large trees that shade the campsites. Abrams Creeks is more suited for tent camping; the sites are small, and the road is not big enough for large or even smaller RVs. If you are looking for quiet and solitude, this is the place.

5 Look Rock, Foothills Parkway

Location: Foothills Parkway.
Sites: 62.
Facilities: Tables, grills, fire rings; flush toilets, dump station; centrally located water.
Fee: $$.
Road conditions: Paved.
Management: Great Smoky Mountains National Park; (865) 436–1230.
Activities: Hiking, sightseeing on the parkway, auto touring.
Season: May–October.
Finding the campground: From Maryville take U.S. Highway 321 north 10 miles to the Foothills Parkway. Turn right onto the parkway and go west 9.3 miles; watch for a sign and turn left onto the road into the campground.

The campground: This campground just has a great feel about it—it's a place to relax, read a book, and listen to the birds sing. Because of its higher elevation, it's cooler in summer; the sites are shady and very natural looking, with large boulders in some of the sites. Look Rock is larger than Abrams Creek, but it, too, is a great place to find peace and quiet. I was there two days before the Fourth of July and about fifteen campsites were occupied. It is sort of out of the way, so it gets fewer visitors than some of the other park campgrounds.

Area 5
Crossville, Oak Ridge, and Wartburg

Oak Ridge is probably the best known town in this area. It is nicknamed "the secret city," because when President Franklin Roosevelt ordered the Manhattan Project, the building of the atomic bomb, Oak Ridge was planned as a city for the workers to live in. The original plan was a town for about 12,000 to 14,000 but grew to 75,000 in three years. The city was opened to the public in 1949 and still remains close to its beginnings—leading the way in research and development in energy, nuclear research, and medical and materials research.

Crossville is what I would call a "large small town." Like a lot of other older towns in our country, it retains some of its past history while at the same time welcoming the future. One of the things that makes Crossville a destination for many people is its golf course. Just outside Crossville, near Cumberland Mountain State Park, is the community of Homestead. Homestead started in the early and mid-1930s to provide the people of Cumberland County with jobs and low-cost housing. Most of the original houses in this area were made with Crab Orchard stone, which was quarried nearby. The Homestead Tower, located in the center of the community, at one time housed the administrative offices for the project. The 85-foot-tall tower was also a water tank that served the surrounding homes. It is now a museum that houses many artifacts from the community's beginnings.

Wartburg is definitely a small town, with only 936 residents and covering four square miles, but it is a wonderful place to visit. The folks here are very welcoming. The town's name came from Wartburg Castle in Germany. The founders were German-speaking immigrants who thought that the area looked like the area around the castle. Today it is best known for its natural beauty and outdoor activities. Just outside town you'll find the Big South Fork National River and Recreation Area, Catoosa Wildlife Management Area, the Obed Wild and Scenic River, and the Cumberland Trail.

For more information:

Oak Ridge Chamber of Commerce
1400 Oak Ridge Turnpike
Oak Ridge, TN 37830
(865) 483–1321
www.orcc.org

Crossville Chamber of Commerce
34 South Main Street
Crossville, TN 38555
(931) 484–8444
(877) 465–3861 (Golf Tennessee)
www.crossville-chamber.com/

Morgan County Chamber of Commerce
P.O. Box 539
Wartburg, TN 37887
(423) 346–5740
www.morgancotn.com

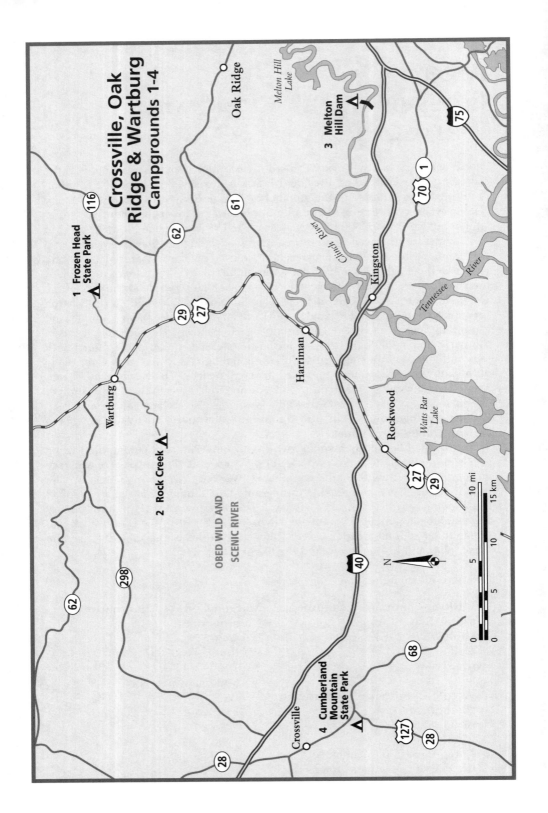

Crossville, Oak Ridge & Wartburg Campgrounds 1-4

1 Frozen Head State Park

2 Rock Creek

3 Melton Hill Dam

4 Cumberland Mountain State Park

Oak Ridge

Melton Hill Lake

Clinch River

Tennessee River

Watts Bar Lake

Kingston

Harriman

Rockwood

Wartburg

OBED WILD AND SCENIC RIVER

Crossville

N

10 mi

15 km

116

62

61

70

1

75

29

27

298

62

40

68

127

28

28

	Group sites	RV sites	Total sites	Max. RV length	Hookups	Toilets	Showers	Drinking water	Dump station	Pets	Wheelchair	Recreation	Fee ($)	Season	Can reserve	Stay limit
1 Frozen Head State Park	•	19	19	36		F	•	•		•	•	HMR	$	March–Nov.		14
2 Rock Creek			12			V			•			SHFKC	$			14
3 Melton Hill Dam		53	53	35		F	•	•	•	•		FSBL	$$			21
4 Cumberland Mountain State Park		147	147	40	EWS	F	•	•	•	•	•	SFH	$–$$			14

Hookups: W = Water E = Electric S = Sewer **Toilets:** F = Flush V = Vault P = Pit C = Chemical **Recreation:** H = Hiking S = Swimming F = Fishing B = Boating L = Boat Launch R = Horseback Riding O = Off-highway driving W = Wildlife watching M = Mountain Biking C = Canoeing G= Golf K = Kayaking **Maximum Trailer/RV length** given in feet. **Stay Limit** given in days. **Fee** given in dollars. If no entry under **Season**, campground is open all year. If no entry under **Fee**, camping is free.

1 Frozen Head State Park

Location: East of Wartburg.
Sites: 19.
Facilities: Tables, grills, fire rings, lantern posts; flush toilets; centrally located water.
Fee: $.
Road conditions: Paved.
Management: Frozen Head State Park; (423) 346–3318.
Activities: Hiking, fishing, mountain biking, playground, horse trails.
Season: March–November.
Finding the campground: From U.S. Highway 27 in Wartburg take Tennessee Highway 62 east 1.9 miles. Turn left onto Flat Fork Road and follow it 3.8 miles to the park entrance; follow signs to the campground.

The campground: This state park's campground is relatively small compared with other state parks. With only nineteen well-spaced-out campsites, camping here is a quiet and relaxing experience. While this campground has no on-site hookups, it does have hot showers. Frozen Head gets its name from 3,324-foot Frozen Head Mountain; the top of this peak is sometimes white from snow or heavy frost while the valley below is not. Not far from the campground you'll find 50 miles of hiking trails, including the Jeep Road Trail. This 6.9-mile trail is used for hiking, mountain biking, and horseback riding. If you want to horseback ride here, you must bring your own horse; there is no place to keep horses overnight. The 11,876 acres that make up this park provide some of the richest wildflower habitat in Tennessee. Peak blooming is sometime in mid-April.

2 Rock Creek, Obed Wild and Scenic River

Location: West of Wartburg.
Sites: 12.
Facilities: Tables, grills, fire rings, lantern posts; vault toilets.

View of Obed Wild and Scenic River

Fee: $.
Road conditions: Paved; dirt in the campground.
Management: Obed Wild and Scenic River, National Park Service; (423) 346–6294.
Activities: Kayaking, canoeing, swimming, hiking, fishing.
Season: Year-round.
Finding the campground: From downtown Wartburg, turn onto Spring Street next to the jail. Spring Street soon becomes Catoosa Road; follow it for 5.8 miles and cross the bridge at the Obed River. Just past the bridge turn right into Rock Creek Campground.

The campground: This is one of the best primitive campgrounds I have ever seen. On my visit the campground was very clean and orderly. Each site was well marked off, with small rustic fences separating the roads from the sites. There is river access right at the campground for kayaks or canoes. Some wonderful hiking trails leave from the campground. The Cumberland Trail, which stretches from Georgia to Kentucky, passes through the campground. The major thing to remember about camping here is that there is no drinking water—so bring plenty.

3 Melton Hill Dam

Location: South of Oak Ridge.

Sites: 53.

Facilities: Tables, lantern posts, grills, tent pads; flush toilets, dump station, showers; centrally located water; beach.

Fee: $$.

Road conditions: Paved.

Management: Tennessee Valley Authority; (865) 988–2432.

Activities: Boating, fishing, swimming, short nature trail.

Season: Open year-round.

Finding the campground: From Interstate 40 west of Knoxville take exit 364 and go north on Tennessee Highway 95 for 0.8 mile. Turn right into the entrance to Melton Hill Dam.

The campground: Melton Hill Dam Campground is a great site for several reasons. For the full-time RV'er it's not far from the interstate for an overnight or few days' stay. For someone wishing to camp but still be able to get to the city, it's only a few miles from Oak Ridge, Knoxville, and Lenoir City. This campground is a great place for fishing enthusiasts, with a boat launch and good clean sites on the water.

This old bridge over the Obed River is now part of the Cumberland Trail.

4 Cumberland Mountain State Park

Location: Crossville.
Sites: 147.
Facilities: Tables, grills, lantern posts; campground store, restaurant, golf; electrical and water hookups, 13 sites with sewer hookups; showers, flush toilets, dump station.
Fee: $-$$.
Road conditions: Paved.
Management: Cumberland Mountain State Park; (800) 250-8618.
Activities: Swimming, fishing, hiking, golf, paddleboats.
Season: Open year-round.
Finding the campground: From downtown Crossville take U.S. Highway 127 south for 3.6 miles, where US 127 turns right. From here go 0.7 mile and turn right onto Tennessee Highway 419 north. This is also the entrance to the park; the campground is 0.2 mile ahead on the right.

The campground: Cumberland Mountain State Park is a very historical area. The park was built by the Civilian Conservation Corps, the Works Project, and the American Friends Service Committee at about the same time as the Homestead Community. The stone bridge and dam that TN 419 crosses is the largest masonry structure ever built by the CCC. The campground here is consistently being improved. There are now thirteen sites with sewer hookups, and they are improving their wheelchair-accessible sites. There is an Olympic-size pool within walking distance of the campground. This seems to be a popular spot for RV'ers.

Area 6

Cherokee National Forest, Southern Districts

The southern districts of the Cherokee National Forest stretch from the southern tip of the Great Smoky Mountains National Park to the Georgia state line and are bordered on the east by North Carolina. This is a vast area of managed forest, scenic drives, mountain peaks, white-water streams, and recreation areas. The opportunities for recreation are endless. Here you can find the Cherohala Skyway, a 43-mile National Scenic Byway that winds its way over mountain peaks between Tellico Plains, Tennessee, and Robbinsville, North Carolina. Some of the best white-water rafting and kayaking in the country are located in the Ocoee District. The beautiful Ocoee Whitewater Center was home to the 1996 Summer Olympic white-water competition. If fishing is more your speed, you'll surely enjoy the Hiwassee and Tellico Rivers; both are popular spots for reeling in large trout. These are just a sampling of outdoor activities in the area; don't forget about hiking, hunting, mountain biking, shooting ranges, boating, water-skiing, nature photography, and wildlife viewing. There is something here for just about everyone.

Within the Tellico Ranger District, in the Tellico River and North River Corridors, there are several designated camping areas. These areas are spread throughout the corridors and are marked with roadside signs. I haven't listed each individual camping area because they are more basic areas where camping is allowed rather than "campgrounds." Some are nothing more than spots in a field, with no marked sites or facilities; others have a portable toilet. Camping here is free. I have seen an area with one person and areas with as many as ten to fifteen different groups camping. These areas give campers another choice in primitive camping.

For more information:

Forest Supervisor Office
2800 North Ocoee Street
P.O. Box 2010
Cleveland, TN 37320
(423) 476–9700

Tellico-Hiwassee Ranger District
250 Ranger Station Road
Tellico Plains, TN 37385
(423) 253–2520

Ocoee-Hiwassee Ranger District
Route 1, Box 3480
Benton, TN 37307
(423) 338–5201

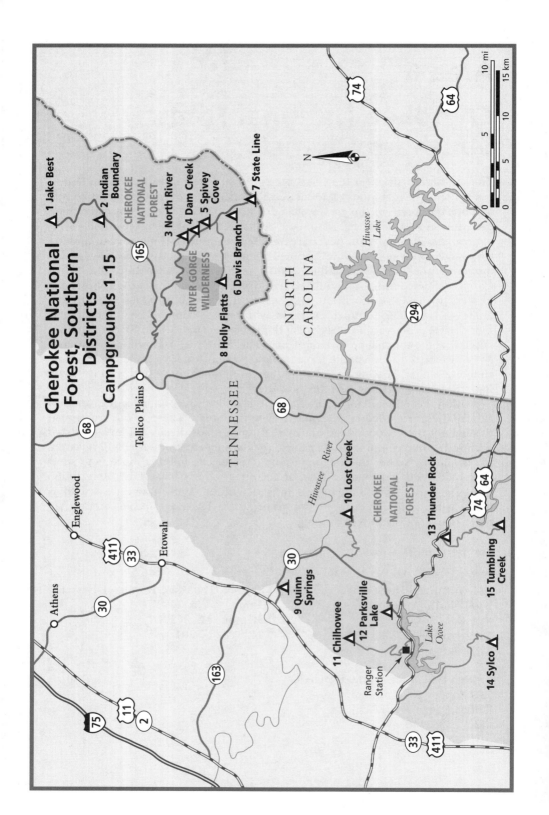

Cherokee National Forest, Southern Districts Campgrounds 1-15

△ 1 Jake Best
△ 2 Indian Boundary
△ 3 North River
△ 4 Dam Creek
△ 5 Spivey Cove
△ 6 Davis Branch
△ 7 State Line
△ 8 Holly Flatts
△ 9 Quinn Springs
△ 10 Lost Creek
△ 11 Chilhowee
△ 12 Parksville Lake
△ 13 Thunder Rock
△ 14 Sylco
△ 15 Tumbling Creek

CHEROKEE NATIONAL FOREST

RIVER GORGE WILDERNESS

CHEROKEE NATIONAL FOREST

TENNESSEE

NORTH CAROLINA

Hiwassee Lake

Hiwassee River

Tellico Plains

Englewood

Athens

Etowah

Ranger Station

Lake Ocoee

N

0   5   10
0   5   10   15 km
10 mi

	Group sites	RV sites	Total sites	Max. RV length	Hookups	Toilets	Showers	Drinking water	Dump station	Pets	Wheelchair	Recreation	Fee ($)	Season	Can reserve	Stay limit
1 Jake Best–Tellico		8	8	30		V				•		FHO	$			14
2 Indian Boundary–Tellico	•	102	102	44	E	F	•	•	•	•	•	FHOLBMS	$-$$	April–Oct.	•	14
3 North River–Tellico		10	10	30		V	•			•		FSMOH	$			14
4 Dam Creek–Tellico			10			V				•		HFSO	$			14
5 Spivey Cove–Tellico			17	20		V				•		FHSMO	$			14
6 Davis Branch–Tellico		4	4	36		V				•		FHOMS	$			14
7 State Line–Tellico		11	11	36		V	•			•		FSHOM	$			14
8 Holly Flatts–Tellico			17	15		V				•		FHS	$			14
9 Quinn Springs–Hiwassee		24	24	30		FV	•	•		•		FCKH	$			14
10 Lost Creek–Hiwassee		2	15	35		V	•		•			F	$			14
11 Chilhowee–Ocoee		25	88	35	E	F	•	•	•	•	•	HSMFCK	$$	April–Oct.		14
12 Parksville Lake–Ocoee	•	17	41	40	E	F	•	•	•	•	•	HFSBLMCK	$$			14
13 Thunder Rock–Ocoee		42	42	35		F	•	•	•	•	•	HKSMC	$			14
14 Sylco–Ocoee			12	20		V				•						14
15 Tumbling Creek–Ocoee	•		8			V				•		FH				14

Hookups: W = Water E = Electric S = Sewer **Toilets:** F = Flush V = Vault P = Pit C = Chemical **Recreation:** H = Hiking S = Swimming F = Fishing B = Boating L = Boat Launch R = Horseback Riding O = Off-road driving W = Wildlife watching M = Mountain Biking C = Canoeing G = Golf K = Kayaking **Maximum Trailer/RV length** given in feet. **Stay Limit** given in days. **Fee** given in dollars. If no entry under **Season**, campground is open all year. If no entry under **Fee**, camping is free.

1 Jake Best

Location: Cherokee National Forest, Tellico District.
Sites: 8.
Facilities: Tables, grills, lantern posts, fire rings; vault toilets.
Fee: $.
Road conditions: Gravel, rough with narrow bridges.
Management: Cherokee National Forest, Tellico Ranger District; (423) 253–2520.
Activities: Fishing, hiking.
Season: Year-round.
Finding the campground: From the junction of Tennessee Highways 68 and 165E, take TN165E 14.3 miles; turn left onto Forest Road 345. Go 1.2 miles and turn right onto gravel Forest Road 35. Follow FR 35 for 2.3 miles to a fork; stay left and go another 5.2 miles. Jake Best is on the right.

The campground: Jake Best is a small but very well kept campground on Citico Creek. Trout fishing is good all up and down Citico Creek. Most people who camp here appear to be either anglers or people looking for solitude. The road into here is gravel and has some narrow bridges, but I saw at least 30-foot RVs at different places on the river.

2 | Indian Boundary

Location: Cherokee National Forest, Tellico District.
Sites: 102.
Facilities: Tables, grills, fire rings, lantern posts; beach; camp store; flush toilets, showers, dump station.
Fee: $-$$.
Road conditions: Paved.
Management: Cherokee National Forest, Tellico Ranger District; (423) 253-2520.
Reservations: (877) 444-6777.
Activities: Fishing, canoeing, hiking, boating, swimming, mountain biking.
Season: April–October; limited camping in winter.
Finding the campground: From the junction of Tennessee Highways 68 and 165E, take TN 165E 14.3 miles; turn left onto Forest Road 345 and go 1.2 miles to the entrance to Indian Boundary Recreation Area.

The campground: This is a beautiful facility. The campground has three large loops; sites on each loop vary from basic to sites with electrical hookups. The ninety-six-acre lake has some great fishing. Bass, bluegill, catfish, and trout can all be caught. Only nonmotorized boats or boats with electric motors are allowed on the lake, which makes for a peaceful fishing experience. There is a wheelchair-accessible fishing pier near Loop A. A 3-mile trail loops around the lake and can be used for either hiking or bicycles. The lake also has a swimming beach for summertime fun. Reservations can be made for Indian Boundary, but after September 25 camping is on a first-come, first-served basis. Winter camping is allowed in the overflow area, but there are no hookups or showers here.

3 | North River

Location: Cherokee National Forest, Tellico District.
Sites: 10.
Facilities: Tables, grills, fire rings, lantern posts; vault toilets.
Fee: $.
Road conditions: Paved and gravel.
Management: Cherokee National Forest, Tellico Ranger District; (423) 252-2520.
Activities: Fishing, swimming, hiking, off-road driving, mountain biking.
Season: Year-round.
Finding the campground: From the junction of Tennessee Highways 68 and 165E, take TN 165E. Go 5.2 miles and turn right onto Forest Road 210; go 9.7 miles and turn left onto Forest Road 217. Go 2.7 miles and the campground is on the right. Most of FR 217 is gravel, but it's smooth and wide.

The campground: This seems to be one of the more popular small campgrounds in Cherokee National Forest. The sites here are very nice, level, smooth, and very large. Like most of the other campgrounds here, this one is next to a stream that is used for swimming at the campground and fishing above and below the campground. On my visit there was one open site, and a couple of sites had an RV and a pop-up camper.

4 Dam Creek

Location: Cherokee National Forest, Tellico District.
Sites: 10.
Facilities: Tables, grills; vault toilets.
Fee: $.
Road conditions: Paved.
Management: Cherokee National Forest, Tellico Ranger District; (423) 253–2520.
Activities: Fishing, hiking, off-road driving nearby.
Season: Year-round.
Finding the campground: From the junction of Tennessee Highways 68 and 165E, take TN 165E. Go 5.2 miles; turn right onto Forest Road 210 and go 12.2 miles. Turn left into the parking area.

The campground: Dam Creek is a dual-purpose area—both a day use picnic area and a walk-in only campground. The campground is primitive; only picnic tables and bear-proof food lockers designate each site. I have never seen anyone camping here, but I'm sure people do. Walking into the area, you first notice the beautiful stonework and the log pavilion that were constructed by the Civilian Conservation Corps in the 1930. These wonderful structures still look fresh and new and stand as a reminder of the hard work that created places we now enjoy. Please take care of areas like this for future generations.

5 Spivey Cove

Location: Cherokee National Forest, Tellico District.
Sites: 17.
Facilities: Tables, grills, fire rings, lantern posts; vault toilets. The water pump located here is not in use; water must be obtained at North River Campground.
Fee: $.
Road conditions: Paved and gravel.
Management: Cherokee National Forest, Tellico Ranger District; (423) 253–2520.
Activities: Fishing, hiking; nearby swimming, off-road driving.
Season: Year-round.
Finding the campground: From the junction of Tennessee Highways 68 and 165E, take TN 165E. Go 5.2 miles and turn right onto Forest Road 210; go 12.8 miles and turn left into the entrance. The road through the campground is gravel and is not recommended for large RVs.

The campground: Spivey Cove is near FR 210 but far enough off the main road so that you feel more in the wilderness. The sites vary in size, but I didn't see many that seemed suitable for large RVs. A couple of sites share a pull-in parking spot, which would be good for a group that wanted to camp together. The gravel road is traveled only by folks camping here and is a good place for kids to ride their bikes. The campground is very shaded and quiet.

6 Davis Branch

Location: Cherokee National Forest, Tellico District.
Sites: 4.
Facilities: Tables, grills, fire rings, lantern posts; vault toilets.
Fee: $.
Road conditions: Paved.
Management: Cherokee National Forest, Tellico Ranger District; (423) 253–2520.
Activities: Fishing, hiking, swimming; nearby off-road driving.
Season: Year-round.
Finding the campground: From the junction of Tennessee Highways 68 and 165E, take TN 165E. Go 5.2 miles; turn right onto Forest Road 210 and go 15.7 miles. The campground is on the left between the road and Tellico River.

The campground: With only four sites, Davis Branch is very limited on space. The camping area is well maintained and clean, but it is basically right on the side of the main road, with the sites only about 20 yards from the road. The sites here are very large and could accommodate a 36-foot or maybe larger RV.

7 State Line

Location: Cherokee National Forest, Tellico District.
Sites: 11.
Facilities: Tables, grills, fire rings, lantern posts; centrally located water; vault toilets.
Fee: $.
Road conditions: Paved.
Management: Cherokee National Forest, Tellico Ranger District; (423) 253–2520.
Activities: Off-road driving, fishing, hiking, mountain biking.
Season: Year-round.
Finding the campground: From the junction of Tennessee Highways 68 and 165E, take TN 165E. Go 5.2 miles; turn right onto Forest Road 210, and go 17.8 miles. The campground is at the end of the road.

The campground: The big draw at this campground is the off-road driving possibilities. Just past the campground is the North Carolina state line and some of the best four-wheel-drive roads and trails in the Southeast. This area is well known in the off-road circuit, and this campground serves as base for many four-wheelers. The sites are very large and shaded.

8 | Holly Flatts

Location: Cherokee National Forest, Tellico District.
Sites: 17.
Facilities: Tables, grills, fire rings; vault toilets.
Fee: $.
Road conditions: Gravel, narrow and winding.
Management: Cherokee National Forest, Tellico Ranger District; (423) 253–2520.
Activities: Fishing, hiking, swimming.
Season: Year-round.
Finding the campground: From the junction of Tennessee Highways 68 and 165E, take TN 165E. Go 5.2 miles; turn right onto Forest Road 210. Go 13.9 miles and turn right onto Forest Road 126; go 5.9 miles and turn left into the campground. FR 126 is gravel and has some potholes, but a passenger car can easily make this drive. Some sections of the road are narrow with sharp curves, so pulling a camper trailer on this road is not recommended.

The campground: This is a very secluded campground, but if you enjoy a deciduous forest drive you'll like this one. Once I made the drive and reached the entrance, I was impressed by the arched stone bridge leading into the campground. It was too bad that the rest of the campground didn't match the bridge. This is not to say this isn't a nice place to camp but only that this was an amazing piece of stonework to be so far back in the woods. The campground itself didn't appear to be heavily used. The sites near the creek were full, but it looked as though the sites away from the water had not been used very much. One spot in the creek is large enough for playing in the water rather than swimming.

9 | Quinn Springs

Location: Cherokee National Forest, Ocoee/Hiwassee District.
Sites: 24.
Facilities: Tables, grills, fire rings; centrally located water; showers, flush and vault toilets.
Fee: $.
Road conditions: Paved.
Management: Cherokee National Forest, Ocoee/Hiwassee Ranger District; (423) 338–5201.
Activities: Fishing, canoeing, kayaking, hiking.
Season: Year-round.
Finding the campground: From the Ocoee Ranger Station take U.S. Highway 64 east 2 miles, and then turn left onto Tennessee Highway 30. Go approximately 11 miles; campground entrance is on the left. Watch for signs.

The campground: Quinn Springs is located just across TN 30 from the Hiwassee River, a well-known trout fishing river. For the weekend fishing enthusiast, this is an ideal base camp. Large oak and hickory trees provide shade and escape from the summer heat. Hiking trails begin right in the campground, as well as the fishing trail next to the Hiwassee River.

10 Lost Creek

Location: Cherokee National Forest, Ocoee/Hiwassee District.
Sites: 15.
Facilities: Tables, fire rings, grills; centrally located water; vault toilets.
Fee: $.
Road conditions: Gravel.
Management: Cherokee National Forest, Ocoee/Hiwassee Ranger District; (423) 338–5201.
Activities: Fishing.
Season: Year-round.
Finding the campground: From Reliance take Tennessee Highway 30 south for 1.6 miles. Turn left onto Forest Road 103 and go 7.2 miles; turn left into campground.

The campground: Lost Creek is another one of Cherokee National Forest's secluded camping areas. It is next to Big Lost Creek and some pretty good trout fishing. Creature comforts are limited here, but the campground is clean and orderly. This is a good place to relax and find solitude.

11 Chilhowee

Location: Cherokee National Forest, Ocoee/Hiwassee District.
Sites: 88.
Facilities: Tables, grills, fire rings, lantern posts; electrical hookups; centrally located water; flush toilets, showers, dump station; beach.
Fee: $$.
Road conditions: Paved, steep.
Management: Cherokee National Forest, Ocoee/Hiwassee Ranger District; (423) 338–5201.
Activities: Hiking, mountain biking, swimming, fishing.
Season: April–October.
Finding the campground: From the Ocoee Ranger Station, take Forest Road 77, which begins next to the entrance to the ranger station. Go 7.3 miles to the campground sign; turn right and go 0.5 mile to campground. Follow the signs.

The campground: Chilhowee has six loops located in two areas, so finding a spot you like shouldn't be hard. Besides being a campground, this is also a day-use area that gets several visitors a day during the summer months. Loops A and B are nearest to seven-acre McKamy Lake and the swimming beach. The dump station is located in Loop D. There are several hiking trails, but what the area is known for is mountain biking. The biking trails vary from an easy quarter mile to some hard-core 3- to 6-mile loops.

Swimming beach on Parksville Lake

12 Parksville Lake

Location: Cherokee National Forest, Ocoee/Hiwassee District.
Sites: 41.
Facilities: Tables, grills, fire rings, lantern posts; electrical hookups, dump station, showers, flush toilets; centrally located water.
Fee: $$.
Road conditions: Paved.
Management: Cherokee National Forest, Ocoee/Hiwassee Ranger District; (423) 338–5201.
Activities: Hiking, fishing, swimming, boating, canoeing, kayaking, mountain biking are all nearby.
Season: Year-round.
Finding the campground: From the Ocoee Ranger Station take U.S. Highway 64 east 2.2 miles. Turn left onto Tennessee Highway 30; the campground is 0.2 mile ahead. Group camping is on the right side of the road; RV camping is on the left.

The campground: Parksville Lake Campground is divided into two sections. One side of the road is for group camping. This side allows for large groups to camp together but without any hookups. There are also different size areas for different size groups. The other side of TN 30 is for family camping. This side is limited to five people per campsite and has electrical hookups. This is the side used by RVs and single families. Both sides have great camping sites that are level and shaded. Not far from the campground are mountain biking trails that lead up to the Chilhowee Campground. A half mile away on US 64 is a swimming beach on Parksville Lake.

13 Thunder Rock

Location: Cherokee National Forest, Ocoee/Hiwassee District.
Sites: 42.
Facilities: Tables, grills, fire rings, lantern posts; flush toilets, showers; centrally located water.
Fee: $.
Road conditions: Paved.
Management: Cherokee National Forest, Ocoee/Hiwassee District; (423) 338–5201.
Activities: Hiking, white-water kayaking, canoeing, rafting, mountain biking, swimming.
Season: Year-round.
Finding the campground: From the Ocoee Ranger Station take U.S. Highway 64 east for 10.8 miles. Turn right at the sign for Ocoee Powerhouse Number 3; cross the bridge and drive around the powerhouse. The campground is on the other side.

The campground: Thunder Rock is the nearest campground to the site of the 1996 Olympic white-water venue. The Whitewater Center is 0.6 mile east on US 64. The center holds several events throughout the year, including many naturalist events, making this campground popular among white-water and outdoor enthusiasts. The campground itself is located next to the Ocoee River. When water is being diverted to produce electricity at the powerhouse, the pools of water left in the river are great for swimming. The showers are new to the campground as of summer 2002. Even though there are no hookups here, there are several sites big enough to accommodate larger RVs.

14 Sylco

Location: Cherokee National Forest, Ocoee/Hiwassee District.
Sites: 12.
Facilities: Tables, grills; vault toilets.
Fee: Free.
Road conditions: Gravel, rough in spots.
Management: Cherokee National Forest, Ocoee/Hiwassee Ranger District; (423) 338–5201.
Activities: Primitive camping.
Season: Year-round.
Finding the campground: From the Ocoee Ranger Station take U.S. High-

way 64 west approximately 3 miles to Cookson Creek Road. Turn left onto Cookson Creek Road, which becomes Forest Road 55; follow the signs 10 miles to the campground.

The campground: This is a primitive campground with no facilities including no water. Sylco is a long way from most other recreation areas in Cherokee National Forest; keep this in mind when planning a camping trip here.

15 Tumbling Creek

Location: Cherokee National Forest, Ocoee/Hiwassee District.
Sites: 8.
Facilities: Tables, grills, lantern posts; vault toilets.
Fee: Free.
Road conditions: Gravel, rough and narrow.
Management: Cherokee National Forest, Ocoee/Hiwassee Ranger District; (423) 338–5201.
Activities: Fishing, hiking.
Season: Year-round.
Finding the campground: From the Ocoee Ranger Station take U.S. Highway 64 east for 10.8 miles. Turn right at the sign for Ocoee Powerhouse 3. Cross the bridge and take Forest Road 45 for 2 miles to Forest Road 221. Go left on FR 221 and travel 6 miles to the campground.

The campground: Tumbling Creek and Sylco are not much different, although there seems to be more to do in the area of Tumbling Creek. Camping is primitive, and the road into the campground is not very wide. It took about thirty minutes each way to reach the campground, so, like Sylco, I wouldn't recommend this campground for those looking to go back and forth to the white-water areas. It is far enough out to get that wilderness feeling.

Area 7
Chattanooga

Chattanooga, the largest city in southeast Tennessee, has done an amazing job of reinventing itself over the past twenty years. Chattanooga was once called "the American city with the worst air quality in the nation," but starting in the early 1980s Chattanooga turned itself around. In February 1998 *Family Fun Magazine* named Chattanooga as "One of America's Top Ten Family Fun Vacation Cities." Today Chattanooga is a vacation destination for many looking for family-oriented fun. This town is packed full of things for the entire family—whether you're into museums, nature centers, theater, art, or aquariums. Chattanooga is home to the world's largest freshwater aquarium, the first place Coca-Cola was bottled, the birthplace of miniature golf, and the location of the steepest passenger incline railway in the country. The city is surrounded by mountains, rivers, and lakes. It's truly a place where there is something for everyone.

For more information:

Chattanooga Area Convention and Visitors Bureau
(800) 322–3344; (423) 756–8687
www.chattanoogafun.com

1 Chester Frost Park

Location: Chickamauga Lake, near Chattanooga.
Sites: 197.
Facilities: Tables, grills, lantern posts; laundry; playground, boat launch, beach; centrally located water; shower, flush toilets, dump station; water and electrical hookups.
Fee: $$.
Road conditions: Paved.
Management: Hamilton County Parks and Recreation; (423) 842–1077.
Activities: Boating, fishing, swimming, bicycling, water-skiing, horseback riding.
Season: Year-round; not all sites open winter months.
Finding the campground: From Tennessee Highway 153 at North Gate Mall, go north on Tennessee Highway 319, also known as Hixson Pike. Take Hixson Pike 4.1 miles and watch for the sign to Chester Frost Park. Turn right onto Gold Point Road and go 2.2 miles to the park and campground entrance.

The campground: This huge park and campground is just outside the Chattanooga metropolitan area. From the campground it's about a ten-minute drive to the downtown area. The campground itself is on sort of an island, surrounded by water and accessed by a narrow strip of land. The camping area

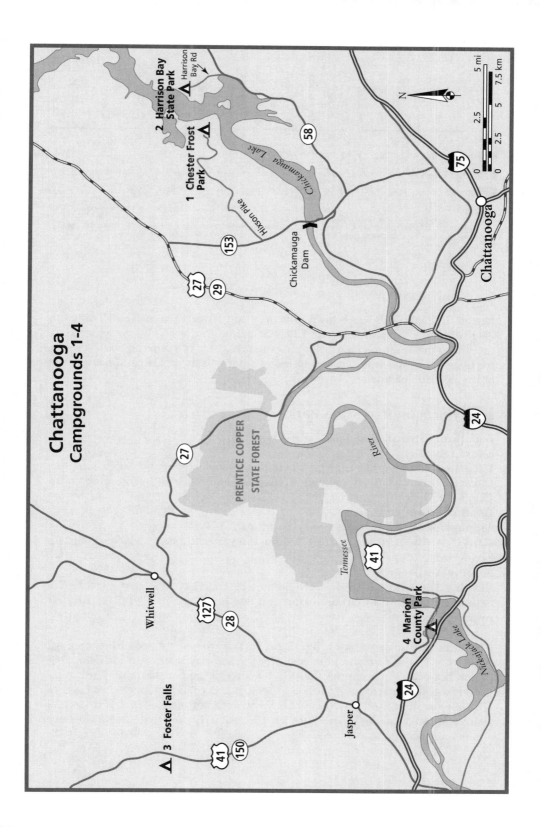

Chattanooga
Campgrounds 1-4

Harrison Bay Rd

2 Harrison Bay State Park

1 Chester Frost Park

Chickamauga Lake

Hixson Pike

58

75

153

Chickamauga Dam

27

29

Chattanooga

PRENTICE COPPER STATE FOREST

27

River

24

Tennessee

41

Whitwell

127

28

4 Marion County Park

24

Nickajack Lake

3 Foster Falls

41

150

Jasper

41

N

0   2.5   5 mi

0   2.5   5   7.5 km

	Group sites	RV sites	Total sites	Max. RV length	Hookups	Toilets	Showers	Drinking water	Dump station	Pets	Wheelchair	Recreation	Fee ($)	Season	Can reserve	Stay limit
1 Chester Frost Park	•	161	197	40	WE	F	•	•	•	•	•	BFSLR	$$			28
2 Harrison Bay State Park	•	82	160	45	WE	F	•	•	•	•	•	BFSHLM	$$			14
3 Foster Falls		26	26	35		F	•	•		•	•	HM	$$	April–Nov.		21
4 Marion County Park		29	29	40	WE	F	•	•		•		FSBL	$$		•	NO LIMIT

Hookups: W = Water E = Electric S = Sewer **Toilets:** F = Flush V = Vault P = Pit C = Chemical **Recreation:** H = Hiking S = Swimming F = Fishing B = Boating L = Boat Launch R = Horseback Riding O = Off-highway driving W = Wildlife watching M = Mountain biking C = Canoeing G = Golf K = Kayaking **Maximum Trailer/RV length** given in feet. **Stay Limit** given in days. **Fee** given in dollars. If no entry under **Season,** campground is open all year. If no entry under **Fee,** camping is free.

is well divided, with tent sites in one area and RV sites in another. There are lakefront sites for both tents and RVs; if being on the lake is not your thing there are sites on the hills overlooking the lake. This is a popular summer spot for boats, personal watercraft, and fishing enthusiasts; boats can be anchored at the lakeside campsites.

2 Harrison Bay State Park

Location: Chickamauga Lake, near Chattanooga.
Sites: 160.
Facilities: Tables, grills, fire rings, lantern posts; electrical and water hookups; showers, flush toilets, dump station; marina and restaurant; swimming pool.
Fee: $$.
Road conditions: Paved.
Management: Harrison Bay State Park; (423) 344–6214.
Activities: Water sports, boating, fishing, hiking, swimming, beach, mountain biking, golf.
Season: Year-round.
Finding the campground: From Tennessee Highways 153 and 58, take TN 58 north 8 miles. Turn left onto Harrison Bay Road and go 1.5 miles; turn left into state park entrance.

The campground: Harrison Bay State Park is due east across Chickamauga Lake from Chester Frost and is basically the same type of camping area. One of the big pluses to camping here is the marina and restaurant. The campground also has a swimming beach as well as a pool. Being located so close to Chattanooga, Harrison Bay fills up early on summer weekends, but it isn't all that crowded weekdays. The sites on the water fill up first. Most sites are shady and have plenty of room.

3 Foster Falls

Location: North of Jasper.
Sites: 26.
Facilities: Tables, grills, fire rings, lantern posts; centrally located water; showers.
Fee: $$.
Road conditions: Paved.
Management: Tennessee Valley Authority; (866) 494-7186.
Activities: Hiking, mountain biking, rock climbing.
Season: April–November.
Finding the campground: From downtown Jasper take U.S. Highway 41 north 8.7 miles. Turn left at the sign for Foster Falls Campground; go 0.4 mile to entrance.

The campground: This is a popular weekend spot among the active crowd, with hiking and rock climbing popular activities. The campground is named for a beautiful waterfall that is within walking distance. The campground is a beautiful facility that is well taken care of by both campers and the folks who manage it. The camping fee is set by the unit; a tent or an RV is a unit, and more than one of either can be on a site.

4 Marion County Park

Location: Southwest of Chattanooga.
Sites: 29.
Facilities: Concrete tables; fishing pier; water and electrical hookups; showers.
Fee: $$.
Road conditions: Paved.
Management: Marion County Parks; (423) 942-6653.
Reservations: (423) 942-6653.
Activities: Fishing, swimming, boating.
Season: Year-round.
Finding the campground: From the junction of Interstate 24 West and Tennessee Highway 156, take TN 156 east 0.9 mile to its intersection with U.S. Highway 41 North. Take US 41 North 1.2 miles and turn left into the campground entrance.

The campground: Its location not far from Interstate 24 makes this campground a likely spot for passing travelers. Surrounded by water, this campground has a fishing pier and boat launch. There's a small, unimproved beach area for swimming. The campground has marked sites for RVs, but tent camping is mostly open and several tents can be placed together. There are showers and rest room facilities, but at the time of my visit they had not been very well kept.

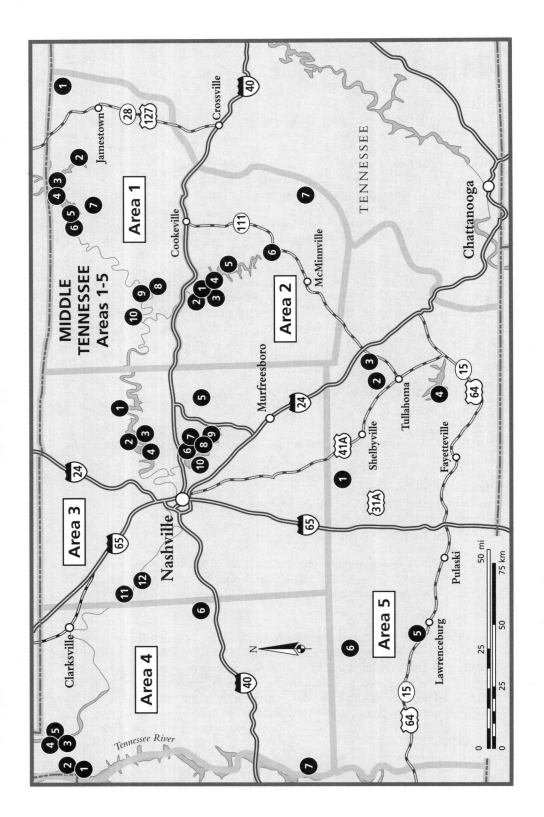

Middle Tennessee

Area 1

Cookeville, Cordell Hull Lake, and Dale Hollow Lake

Cookeville is neither a large city nor a small town, but it has the feel of both. Cookeville, a college town with a population of 26,000, is home to Tennessee Tech University (enrollment 8,600). It is conveniently located near Interstate 40, the major east-west route across the state; Nashville is 79 miles west and Knoxville is 101 miles east. Cookeville is ranked ninth in the nation by Rand McNally's *Places Rated Retirement Guide* and in 1988 was voted as one of "America's Most Affordable Cities" by *USA Today*. Both Cordell Hull and Dale Hollow Lakes are within an hour's drive of Cookeville.

Cordell Hull and Dale Hollow Lakes are owned and managed by the U.S. Army Corps of Engineers. Many of the campgrounds in Middle Tennessee are Corps of Engineers' properties, and they are some of the best campgrounds in the area. Dale Hollow, in the upper corner of this area near the Tennessee and Kentucky state line, is famous for its clean water and great fishing. Some of the best fishing here is below the dam in the tail water, where trout are stocked each week. Cordell Hull Lake is slightly west of Cookeville; it's a smaller reservoir than Dale Hollow but with equally beautiful scenery and good fishing. Several of the U.S. Army Corps of Engineers campgrounds accept reservations; for faster service please use the reservation code next to the phone number if one is provided.

For more information:

Cookeville Chamber of Commerce
302 South Jefferson Avenue
Cookeville, TN 38501
(931) 526-2211
(800) 264-5541
www.cookevillechamber.com

Cordell Hull fishing information:
(615) 735-1050

Dale Hollow fishing information:
(931) 243-3408

73

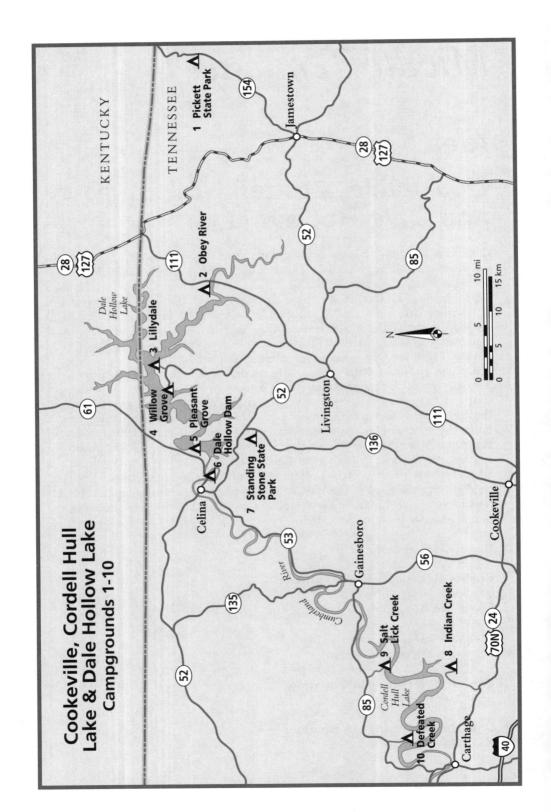

Cookeville, Cordell Hull
Lake & Dale Hollow Lake
Campgrounds 1-10

1 Pickett State Park

Location: North of Jamestown.
Sites: 40.
Facilities: Water and electric hookups, dump station; flush toilets, showers; swimming pool; grills and tables.
Fee: $$.
Road conditions: Paved.
Management: Pickett State Park; (931) 879–5821.
Activities: Hiking, swimming, rowboats.
Season: Year-round.
Finding the campground: From Jamestown take Tennessee Highway 154 north for 15 miles. The entrance to the state park and campground is on the left.

The campground: Pickett State Park, 17,372 acres of natural wonder, is best known for its geological features. The park is located next door to the Big South Fork National River and Recreation Area, and it contains numerous natural bridges and caves. The campground at Pickett State Park is a great place for a base camp from which to explore either Pickett or Big South Fork. The sites here are smaller and suited more to tents, pop-up campers, and small pull trailers.

Ranger Station, Pickett State Park

	Group sites	RV sites	Total sites	Max. RV length	Hookups	Toilets	Showers	Drinking water	Dump station	Pets	Wheelchair	Recreation	Fee ($)	Season	Can reserve	Stay limit
1 Pickett State Park			40	22	EW	F	•	•	•	•		HSB	$$		•	14
2 Obey River		50	132	36	EW	F	•	•	•	•	•	FBLS	$$–$$$	April–Oct.	•	14
3 Lillydale		58	114	40	EW	F	•	•	•	•	•	FBLSH	$–$$$	May–Oct.	•	14
4 Willow Grove		68	83	40	EW	F	•	•	•	•	•	SFHLB	$–$$$	May–Sept.	•	14
5 Pleasant Grove			29			F	•			•	•	SBLF	$	May–Sept.	•	14
6 Dale Hollow Dam		79	79	40	EW	F	•	•	•	•	•	FHBC	$$	April–Nov.	•	14
7 Standing Stone State Park		38	38	36	EW	F	•	•	•	•	•	FHBS	$$		•	14
8 Indian Creek		53	53	45	EW	F	•	•	•	•	•	SFBL	$$	May–Sept.	•	14
9 Salt Lick Creek		150	150	36	EWS	F	•	•	•	•	•	SFBL	$–$$$	May–Sept.	•	14
10 Defeated Creek		150	155	40	EWS	F	•	•	•	•	•	FBLS	$–$$$	April–Oct.	•	14

Hookups: W = Water E = Electric S = Sewer **Toilets:** F = Flush V = Vault P = Pit C= Chemical **Recreation:** H = Hiking S = Swimming F = Fishing B = Boating L = Boat Launch R = Horseback Riding O = Off-highway driving W = Wildlife watching M = Mountain biking C = Canoeing G = Golf K = Kayaking **Maximum Trailer/RV length** given in feet. **Stay Limit** given in days. **Fee** given in dollars. If no entry under **Season**, campground is open all year. If no entry under **Fee**, camping is free.

2 Obey River

Location: Dale Hollow Lake.
Sites: 132.
Facilities: Water and electric hookups, dump station; flush toilets, showers; laundry; boat launch; tables and grills.
Fee: $$–$$$.
Road conditions: Paved.
Management: U.S. Army Corps of Engineers; (931) 864–6388.
Reservations: (877) 444–6777; www.ReserveUSA.com. Reservation code: OBEY.
Activities: Fishing, boating, water-skiing, swimming, playground.
Season: April–October.
Finding the campground: From the junction of Tennessee Highways 52 and 111, take TN 111 north 1.5 miles; TN 111 will turn left. Continue on TN 111 for 13 miles; the entrance to the campground is on the left.

The campground: Obey is a large campground on the shore of Dale Hollow Lake. Its location near TN 111 makes this a very accessible campground. A commercial marina and restaurant are located near the entrance to Obey Campground, so this is not a wilderness experience. But it is a great location for fishing and family fun. This is a good, clean campground with plenty of large, level sites.

3 Lillydale

Location: Dale Hollow Lake.
Sites: 114.
Facilities: Water and electric hookups, dump station; flush toilets, showers; laundry; boat launch, beach; tables, grills, lantern poles, fire rings.
Fee: $–$$$.
Road conditions: Paved.
Management: U.S. Army Corps of Engineers; (931) 823–4155.
Reservations: (877) 444–6777; www.ReserveUSA.com. Reservation code: LILL.
Activities: Fishing, boating, water-skiing, hiking, volleyball, beach, swimming.
Season: May–October.
Finding the campground: From the junction of Tennessee Highways 52W and 111N/294 in Livingston, take TN 111N/294 north for 1.7 miles. TN 111N/294 turns left; go 3.7 miles, where TN 294 turns left. From here TN 294 is also known as Willow Grove Road. Follow Willow Grove Road for 13.8 miles, and turn right onto Lillydale Road. Go 0.9 mile to the campground.

The campground: This campground has many of the same features as other nearby campgrounds, but Lillydale also has a walk-in, tent-only section located on a small island. I found this area to be a real plus if you are looking for a simpler brand of camping. Due to infestation by the pine beetle, Lillydale has lost many large pine trees, leaving the campsites more open. I was very impressed with this very clean and well-groomed campground.

4 Willow Grove

Location: Dale Hollow Lake.
Sites: 83.
Facilities: Water and electric hookups, dump station; flush toilets, showers; laundry; boat launch, beach; tables, grills, lantern poles, fire rings.
Fee: $–$$$.
Road conditions: Paved.
Management: U.S. Army Corps of Engineers; (931) 823–4285.
Reservations: (877) 444–6777; www.ReserveUSA.com. Reservation code: WIGR.
Activities: Fishing, boating, water-skiing, hiking, beach, swimming, volleyball.
Season: May–September.
Finding the campground: From the junction of Tennessee Highways 52W and 111N/294 in Livingston, take TN 111N/294 north for 1.7 miles. TN 111N/294 turns left; go 3.7 miles, where TN 294 turns left. From here TN 294 is also known as Willow Grove Road. Follow Willow Grove Road for 16 miles to the campground entrance.

The campground: Willow Grove is a beautiful campground, with sites that vary from hilltop spots overlooking Dale Hollow Lake to sites that are closer to the water. Some sites are in the open; others are shaded by large hardwood trees. An 8-mile hiking trail, the Accordion Bluff Nature Trail, connects Willow Grove and Lillydale Campgrounds.

5 Pleasant Grove

Location: Dale Hollow Lake.
Sites: 29.
Facilities: Flush toilets; centrally located drinking water; boat launch; tables, grills.
Fee: $.
Road conditions: Paved.
Management: U.S. Army Corps of Engineers; (931) 243-3136.
Activities: Fishing, boating, water-skiing, swimming.
Season: May–September.
Finding the campground: From the junction of Tennessee Highways 52W and 53N in Celina, take TN 53N 4 miles. Turn right onto East Old Fifty Three Road and go 0.7 mile. Turn right onto Cedar Hill Road and go 0.7 mile to Cedar Hill Resort. Stay on the road, bearing right; go 0.5 mile to the Pleasant Grove entrance.

Crossing the bridge to Pleasant Grove Campground

The campground: Pleasant Grove Campground is located on an island in Dale Hollow Lake and can be accessed either by boat or by hiking the 0.25- to 0.5-mile trail. The trail crosses a 100-foot suspension bridge connecting the island with the shore. The twenty-nine campsites on the island are spread out, with plenty of space between. If you come by boat, your boat can be moored at your site and launched from the parking area where the trail starts. This appears to be a popular destination during summer.

6 Dale Hollow Dam

Location: Dale Hollow Lake.
Sites: 79.
Facilities: Water and electric hookups, dump station; flush toilets, showers; laundry; fish-cleaning stations; tables, fire rings, grills, lantern poles.
Fee: $$.
Road conditions: Paved.
Management: U.S. Army Corps of Engineers; (931) 243–3554.
Reservations: (877) 444–6777; www.ReserveUSA.com. Reservation code: DALH.

Trout fishing near the campground at Dale Hollow Dam

Activities: Fishing, boat launch, canoeing, volleyball.
Season: April–November.
Finding the campground: From the junction of Tennessee Highways 52W and 53N in Celina, take TN 53N north 3.7 miles and turn right onto Dale Hollow Dam Road. Go 0.4 mile and turn right onto Campground Road; it's another 0.2 mile to the campground.

The campground: This is one of the Corps of Engineers' most popular campgrounds for several reasons. The campground is extremely clean and well kept, with excellent rest rooms and shower facilities. The area is peaceful. But one of the main reasons is the trout fishing. This campground is located below Dale Hollow Dam, where the Obey River flows from the bottom of the dam. The temperature of the stream water is a constant 45 to 47 degrees Fahrenheit, making it great for trout, which are stocked every Friday. There are two fish-cleaning stations with stainless steel sinks and running water—a great setup for cleaning your catch. Nearby is a boat launch ramp, but I would call before bringing a boat; the stream doesn't appear large enough for a very big one.

7 Standing Stone State Park

Location: Northwest of Livingston.
Sites: 38.
Facilities: Water and electric hookups, dump station; flush toilets, showers; swimming pool; tables, fire rings, lantern poles, grills.
Fee: $$.
Road conditions: Paved.
Management: Standing Stone State Park; (931) 823–6347 or (800) 713–5157.
Activities: Hiking, boating, swimming, fishing.
Season: Year-round.
Finding the campground: From the junction of Tennessee Highways 111 and 52 in Livingston, take TN 52 north for 8.6 miles. Turn left onto Tennessee Highway 136 south; go 1.2 miles to the campground entrance on the left.

The campground: This state park campground is smaller than most other state park campgrounds, but sometimes smaller is good. On the weekend that I visited, the campground wasn't crowded, which makes for a peaceful camping experience. The sites are shaded by large hardwood trees and have plenty of room for RVs or tents. Standing Stone State Park has its own small lake, but you could also camp here and drive to Dale Hollow Lake to fish.

8 Indian Creek

Location: Cordell Hull Lake.
Sites: 53.
Facilities: Water and electric hookups, dump station; flush toilets, showers; laundry; beach; tables, fire rings, grills.
Fee: $$.
Road conditions: Paved.

Management: U.S. Army Corps of Engineers; (931) 897–2233.
Reservations: (877) 444–6777; www.ReserveUSA.com.
Activities: Fishing, boating, water-skiing, swimming.
Season: May–September.
Finding the campground: From Carthage take U.S. Highway 70 east 8.9 miles and turn left onto Tennessee Highway 53 east. Go 2.6 miles and turn right onto Enigma Road; go 2.3 miles and turn left onto Webster Road. Follow Webster Road 0.7 mile to campground entrance.

The campground: Indian Creek is a smaller campground, with only fifty-three sites. It appears that this is a less-crowded area, which may be because this campground is not on the main channel of Cordell Hull Lake. This is a very clean and well-maintained camping area. Thirty-two sites have water and electrical hookups.

9 Salt Lick Creek

Location: Cordell Hull Lake.
Sites: 150.
Facilities: Water, electric, and some sewer hookups, dump station; flush toilets, showers; laundry; tables, fire rings, grills, lantern poles.
Fee: $–$$$.
Road conditions: Paved.
Management: U.S. Army Corps of Engineers; (931) 638–4718.
Reservations: (877) 444–6777; www.ReserveUSA.com.
Activities: Fishing, boating, water-skiing, beach, swimming, playground.
Season: May–September.
Finding the campground: From downtown Gainesboro take East Hull Avenue 0.7 mile and turn right onto Tennessee Highways 262 and 85 west. Go 9.4 miles and turn left onto Smith Bend Road. Go 1 mile and make a right turn onto Salt Lick Park Lane; go 0.8 mile to the campground.

The campground: This is a beautiful campground with lots of sites shaded by hardwood trees and large grassy areas between sites that are very well manicured. Official word is that a 36-foot RV is the maximum length, but several of the sites would hold larger models. The sites near the water gently slope to the water's edge but are very level nonetheless. The sites that are not on the water have the feel of being in the woods.

10 Defeated Creek

Location: Cordell Hull Lake.
Sites: 155.
Facilities: Water, electric, and some sewer hookups, dump station; flush toilets, showers; laundry; tables, grills, fire rings, lantern poles.
Fee: $–$$$.
Road conditions: Paved.
Management: U.S. Army Corps of Engineers; (615) 774–3141.

Reservations: (877) 444–6777; www.ReserveUSA.com.
Activities: Fishing, boating, water-skiing, beach, swimming, playground.
Season: April–October.
Finding the campground: From the intersection of Tennessee Highways 25 and 263 in Carthage, take TN 263 north 5.1 miles. Turn right onto Tennessee Highway 85 east; go 2 miles and turn right onto Marina Lane. Go 1.4 miles to the campground entrance.

The campground: Defeated Creek is another great Corps of Engineers campground. This is a good spot for fishing, boating, or just relaxing. The Corps really knows how to plan out a campground—and how to maintain it. Sixty-three of the sites have sewer hookups, and all have water and electricity. The sites are large, with plenty of shade, and a commercial marina and restaurant are just outside the campground. A secure parking area is provided for boat trailers, which creates extra room at the sites.

Area 2

Center Hill Lake, McMinnville, and Smithville

Center Hill Lake is the largest of the U.S. Army Corps of Engineers lakes in Tennessee, covering 18,200 acres. It's also one of the most popular recreation destinations in Middle Tennessee—with good reason. Hiking, fishing, swimming, boating, and many other water sports are enjoyed on Center Hill's beautiful water.

Not far south of Center Hill Lake is the town of McMinnville, with Rock Island and Fall Creek Falls State Parks both nearby. McMinnville, the largest town in this area of Tennessee, is known as "The Nursery Capital of the World." The local chamber of commerce lists forty-two plant nurseries as members, and I know there must be many more. The fields are covered with growing trees and flowers. The fertile soil and 53 inches of rain annually make McMinnville a great spot for growing plants—and a great place to visit in spring and early summer, when the flowers are in bloom.

Located closer to Center Hill Lake is Smithville and its world-famous Fiddlers Jamboree, a music and craft festival, but this is no ordinary festival. Smithville, a small town of around 4,000 persons, grows to around 80,000 during the first weekend in July. In 1992 *Vacation Magazine* rated the jamboree the fourth best event in the United States to attend on a summer vacation. Each year, visitors from all fifty states and several foreign countries spend their vacations at the festival.

For more information:

McMinnville Chamber of Commerce
110 South Court Square
McMinnville, TN 37111
(931) 473–6611
www.warrentn.com

Smithville-Dekalb County Chamber of Commerce
P.O. Box 64
Smithville, TN 37166
(615) 597–4163
www.smithvilletn.com

Fishing Information Hot Line
(931) 858–4366
(615) 548–8581

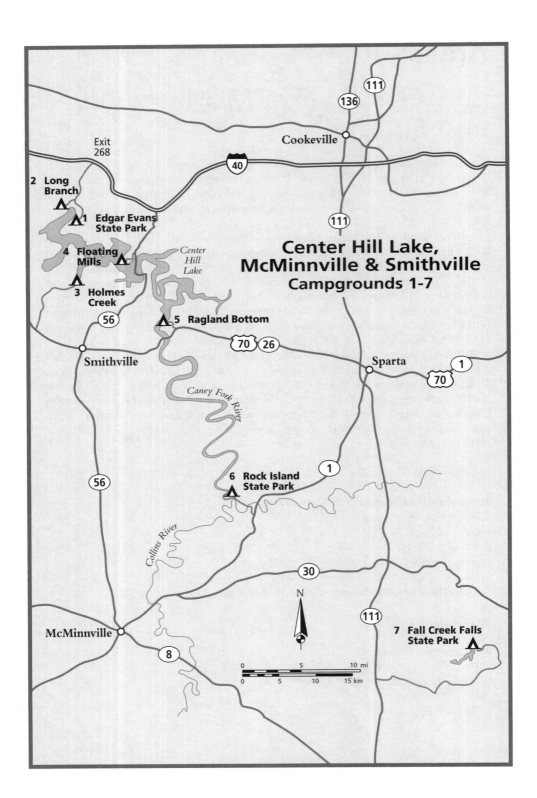

	Group sites	RV sites	Total sites	Max. RV length	Hookups	Toilets	Showers	Drinking water	Dump station	Pets	Wheelchair	Recreation	Fee ($)	Season	Can reserve	Stay limit
1 Edgar Evans State Park		60	60	40	EW	F	•	•	•	•	•	SBLFH	$$			14
2 Long Branch		60	60	45	EW	F	•	•	•	•	•	FC	$$	April–Oct.	•	14
3 Holmes Creek		22	97	36	EW	F	•	•	•	•		BFL	$$	May–Sept.	•	14
4 Floating Mills		66	118	40	EW	F	•	•	•	•	•	LFBHS	$$	April–Oct.	•	14
5 Ragland Bottom		30	56	40	EWS	F	•	•	•	•	•	HFSBL	$$	May–Oct.	•	14
6 Rock Island State Park		50	60	45	EW	F	•	•	•	•	•	HFBS	$$		•	14
7 Fall Creek Falls State Park	•		228		EWS	F	•	•	•	•	•	HFBSRC	$$		•	14

Hookups: W = Water E = Electric S = Sewer **Toilets:** F = Flush V = Vault P = Pit C = Chemical **Recreation:** H = Hiking S = Swimming F = Fishing B = Boating L = Boat Launch R = Horseback Riding O = Off-highway driving W = Wildlife watching M = Mountain biking C = Canoeing G = Golf K = Kayaking **Maximum Trailer/RV length** given in feet. **Stay Limit** given in days. **Fee** given in dollars. If no entry under **Season**, campground is open all year. If no entry under **Fee**, camping is free.

1 Edgar Evans State Park

Location: Center Hill Lake.
Sites: 60.
Facilities: Water and electric hookup, dump station; flush toilets, showers; laundry; tables, grills, fire rings; nearby commercial marina.
Fee: $$.
Road conditions: Paved.
Management: Edgar Evans State Park; (931) 858–2446.
Activities: Hiking, fishing, swimming, boating, water-skiing, playground.
Season: Year-round.
Finding the campground: From Interstate 40 west of Cookeville, take exit 268 to Tennessee Highway 96. Go south 3.6 miles to Tennessee Highway 141. The entrance to Edgar Evans State Park is directly across TN 141.

The campground: This is the most unusual campground layout that I have ever seen, but it is also one of the best concepts I have ever seen. All sixty sites here are on platforms that resemble a patio deck. The platforms are built on a hillside using concrete pillars and steel I beams to create a strong structure that is then covered with wood. The strength is apparent when large RVs are parked on them. I wasn't sure about this idea at first, but after talking with several campers I found that most like the concept. It is a great use of a hillside; when it rains, the water drains off quickly and there is never any mud—and all sites are level.

Relaxing on one of the camping platforms at Edgar Evans State Park

2 Long Branch

Location: Center Hill Lake.
Sites: 60.
Facilities: Water and electric hookups, dump station; flush toilets, showers; laundry; tables, grills, fire rings, lantern poles.
Fee: $$.
Road conditions: Paved.
Management: U.S. Army Corps of Engineers; (615) 548-8002.
Reservations: (877) 444-6777; www.ReserveUSA.com.
Activities: Fishing, canoeing, nearby hiking at Edgar Evans State Park.
Season: April-October.
Finding the campground: From Interstate 40 west of Cookeville, take exit 268 to Tennessee Highway 96. Go south 3.6 miles to Tennessee Highway 141 and turn right (TN 96 and TN 141 are combined here). Go 1.1 miles; cross the dam and turn right onto TN 141 west. Go 0.3 mile and turn right into the campground entrance.

The campground: Long Branch is located next to Caney Fork River, just below Center Hill Dam. This campground is a mixture of shady and open sites, but all are level and have wooden tables for cleaning fish. The trout fishing here seems to be fairly good and is one of the campground draws. The area is also a good spot to base a canoeing or kayaking trip on the Caney River. About a half mile away is a public boat launch on Center Hill Lake.

3 Holmes Creek

Location: Center Hill Lake.
Sites: 97.
Facilities: Water and electric hookups, dump station; flush toilets, showers; laundry; playground; tables, grills, lantern posts.
Fee: $$.
Road conditions: Paved.
Management: U.S. Army Corps of Engineers; (615) 597–7191.
Reservations: (877) 444–6777; www.ReserveUSA.com.
Activities: Boating, fishing, water-skiing.
Season: May–September.
Finding the campground: From the junction of U.S. Highway 70 and Tennessee Highway 56 in Smithville, take US 70 west for 3.5 miles. Turn right onto Casey Cove Road and go 5.2 miles to the campground entrance. The last 2 miles are a very steep hill.

The campground: Holmes Creek Campground is on Holmes Creek, a tributary of Center Hill Lake. Several sites are at the water's edge but not down level with the water; they lie more above the shore, with steep, rocky slopes to the water. The rest of the sites are on the hillside above the lake. I really like these hillside sites; they have more of a rustic in-the-woods feel. There are some grassy areas in the campground but none is like a manicured lawn. This area of Tennessee is very rocky, and it is especially apparent here.

4 Floating Mills

Location: Center Hill Lake.
Sites: 118.
Facilities: Water and electric hookups, dump station; flush toilets, showers; laundry; tables, grills, fire rings.
Fee: $$.
Road conditions: Paved.
Management: U.S. Army Corps of Engineers; (615) 858–4845.
Reservations: (877) 444–6777; www.ReserveUSA.com.
Activities: Fishing, boating, water-skiing, swimming, hiking.
Season: April–October.
Finding the campground: From the junction of Tennessee Highway 56 and U.S. Highway 70 in Smithville, take TN 56 north for 9.6 miles. Turn left onto Floating Mills Road and go 0.7 mile to the three forks in the road; take the middle fork and follow this to the campground.

The campground: Floating Mills is located in the rolling hills on the shore of Center Hill Lake. The 118 sites make this a fairly large campground, and its location close to a main road makes it a popular spot. Some of the sites here are close together, but most have enough room for the average camper. The campground has a nice beach area for swimming and a short hiking trail that connects to a day-use area. This is a great location to camp while visiting Smithville.

5 Ragland Bottom

Location: Center Hill Lake.
Sites: 56.
Facilities: Water, electric, and some sewer hookups, dump station; flush toilets, showers; laundry; tables, grills, fire rings, lantern poles.
Fee: $$.
Road conditions: Paved.
Management: U.S. Army Corps of Engineers; (615) 761–3616.
Reservations: (877) 444–6777; www.ReserveUSA.com.
Activities: Hiking, swimming, beach, fishing, boating, water-skiing, basketball, volleyball, playground.
Season: May–October.
Finding the campground: From the junction of U.S. Highway 70 and Tennessee Highway 56 in Smithville, take US 70 east 7.1 miles. Turn left onto Ragland Bottom Road, and go 1.4 miles to the campground entrance.

The campground: The lakeside sites here are very nice and accessible to the water. These sites are also very large; some are 120 feet long. The sites away from the water are smaller, but several are pull-through sites. There is plenty of shade from hardwood trees and lots of lawn space between sites. Ten of the sites have sewer hookups.

6 Rock Island State Park

Location: Northeast of McMinnville.
Sites: 60.
Facilities: Water and electric hookups, dump station; flush toilets, showers; tables, grills, fire rings; playground.
Fee: $$.
Road conditions: Paved.
Management: Rock Island State Park; (931) 686–2471.
Reservations: (800) 713–6065; $5.00 reservation fee.
Activities: Hiking, fishing, swimming, beach, boating.
Season: Year-round.
Finding the campground: From the junction of U.S. Highway 70 and Tennessee Highway 56 in McMinnville, take US 70 east for 12 miles. Turn left onto Tennessee Highway 136 north; go 1.2 miles and turn left onto Tennessee Highway 287 south. Go 2.2 miles and turn right into park entrance; follow signs to campground.

The campground: The campground is just a short distance from the Caney Fork River, and just another short distance upstream the river is dammed to create Great Falls Lake. Both the lake and the river are good fishing areas. Most of the campsites have a concrete pad around the table and a paved pull-in spot, making the campsites easier to maintain and keep clean.

7 | Fall Creek Falls State Park

Location: South of Cookeville.

Sites: 228.

Facilities: Water, electric, and some sewer hookups, dump station; flush toilets, showers; laundry; tables, grills, fire rings, lantern poles; nearby camp store.

Fee: $$.

Road conditions: Paved.

Management: Fall Creek Falls State Park.

Reservations: (800) 250–8611; $10 reservation fee, with two-night minimum.

Activities: Hiking, boating, canoeing, biking, horseback riding, golf, swimming.

Season: Year-round.

Finding the campground: From the junction of U.S. Highway 70 and Tennessee Highway 111 in Sparta, go south on TN 111 approximately 22 miles. Turn left onto Tennessee Highway 284 and follow the large brown signs into the park.

The campground: Fall Creek Falls is the crown jewel of the Tennessee State Park System. It is a large park at 22,000 acres, and the campground is also large. With 228 sites, there is sure to be one that you like. Just about all the sites have shade, and most are level. Hiking trails lead out from the campground to several areas of the park, which is well known for its waterfalls, including Fall Creek Falls; at 256 feet it's the tallest free-falling waterfall east of the Mississippi. This is a popular park—reservations are recommended on weekends during the summer months.

Area 3

Nashville

Nashville, the state capital of Tennessee, is probably best known as the country music capital of the world. But while most people do associate country music and Nashville, there is so much more than that. Galleries, museums, historical sites, the Grand Ole Opry, hockey, football, baseball, zoos, and gardens all add to the diversity of this metropolitan area. Several of the campgrounds in this section are just a few miles outside Nashville, making them a good base for a vacation to the Music City. The rest of the campgrounds listed are within an hour's drive of downtown.

For more information:

Nashville Convention & Visitors Bureau
(800) 657–6910
www.nashvillecvb.com

J. Percy Priest Lake information:
(615) 883–2351

1 Bledsoe Creek State Park

Location: East of Gallatin.
Sites: 114.
Facilities: Electric and water hookups, dump station; flush toilets, showers; boat launch; tables, grills.
Fee: $$.
Road conditions: Paved.
Management: Bledsoe Creek State Park; (615) 452–3706.
Activities: Hiking, boating, fishing.
Season: Year-round.
Finding the campground: From Gallatin travel east on Tennessee Highway 25 approximately 4.5 miles and turn right onto Zieglers Fort Road. Go 1.3 miles; the park entrance is on the left.

The campground: At the time of my visit, the campground was in need of general maintenance and upkeep. The sites are smaller and will accommodate smaller campers and RVs. There is plenty of room and shade for each site. The park itself has opportunities for hiking, boating, and fishing.

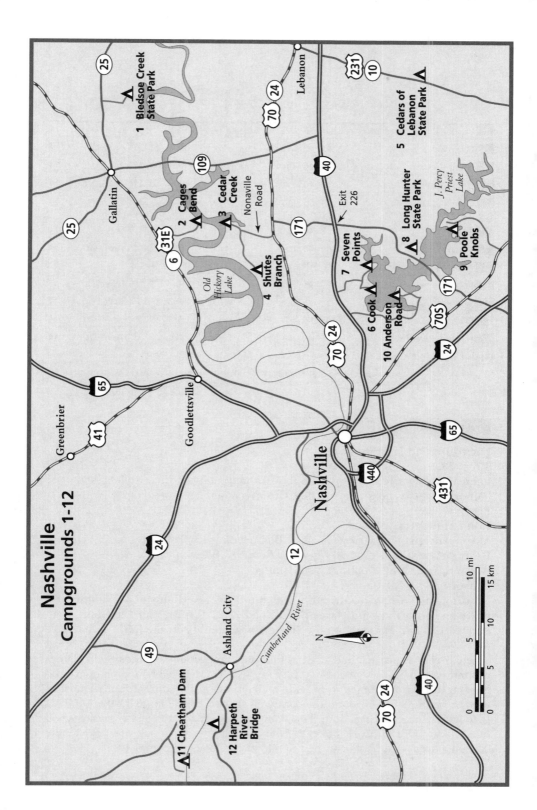

Nashville
Campgrounds 1-12

	Group sites	RV sites	Total sites	Max. RV length	Hookups	Toilets	Showers	Drinking water	Dump station	Pets	Wheelchair	Recreation	Fee ($)	Season	Can reserve	Stay limit
1 Bledsoe Creek State Park		26	114	36	EW	F	•	•	•	•	•	HFBL	$$			14
2 Cages Bend		43	43	45	EW	F	•	•	•	•	•	BFSL	$$–$$$	April–Nov.	•	14
3 Cedar Creek		60	60	40	EW	F	•	•	•	•		BFSL	$$–$$$	Mar.–Oct.	•	14
4 Shutes Branch	•	17	34	40	EW	F	•	•	•	•		BF	$$–$$$	May–Oct.	•	14
5 Cedars of Lebanon State Park	•	87	117	36	EW	F	•	•	•	•	•	SRMH	$$			14
6 Cook		57	57	40		F	•	•	•	•		BFSL	$$	May–Sept.	•	14
7 Seven Points		60	60	40	EW	F	•	•	•	•	•	BSFL	$$–$$$	April–Oct.	•	14
8 Long Hunter State Park	•											BFSHLC	$–$$$		•	NA
9 Poole Knobs	•	84	90	45	EW	F	•	•	•	•	•	BF	$–$$$	May–Sept.	•	14
10 Anderson Road		37	37	35		F	•	•	•	•		HFSBL	$$	May–Sept.	•	14
11 Cheatham Dam		36	45	45	EW	F	•	•	•	•	•	HSFBL	$$	April–Oct.	•	14
12 Harpeth River Bridge	•	15	15	40		V				•		FLC	$	April–Oct.		14

Hookups: W = Water E = Electric S = Sewer **Toilets:** F = Flush V = Vault P = Pit C = Chemical **Recreation:** H = Hiking S = Swimming F = Fishing B = Boating L = Boat Launch R = Horseback Riding O = Off-highway driving W = Wildlife watching M = Mountain Biking C = Canoeing G = Golf K = Kayaking **Maximum Trailer/RV length** given in feet. **Stay Limit** given in days. **Fee** given in dollars. If no entry under **Season**, campground is open all year. If no entry under **Fee**, camping is free.

2 Cages Bend

Location: Old Hickory Lake.
Sites: 43.
Facilities: Electric and water hookups, dump station; flush toilets, showers; laundry; boat launch; tables, grills, fire rings, lantern poles.
Fee: $$–$$$.
Road conditions: Paved.
Management: U.S. Army Corps of Engineers; (615) 824–4989.
Reservations: (877) 444–6777; www.ReserveUSA.com.
Activities: Fishing, boating, water-skiing.
Season: April–November.
Finding the campground: From Gallatin take U.S. Highway 31E south for 5 miles and turn left onto Cages Bend Road. Go 2.9 miles; turn left onto Benders Ferry Road and go 0.4 mile. The campground is on the left.

The campground: If I had a list of favorite campgrounds, Cages Bend Campground would be very near the top of my list. The managers and campground host go the extra distance to provide a clean, beautiful campground. The sites are big, with plenty of room; they are well shaded by the large hardwood trees throughout the campground. The campground is located on a grassy knoll overlooking Old Hickory Lake. A boat launch site and dock are next to the camping area, and boats can be moored at the lakeside campsites.

Waterfront sites at Cages Bend

3 Cedar Creek

Location: Old Hickory Lake.
Sites: 60.
Facilities: Electric and water hookups, dump station; showers, flush toilets; laundry; boat launch, beach; tables, grills, fire rings, lantern poles.
Fee: $$–$$$.
Road conditions: Paved.
Management: U.S. Army Corps of Engineers; (615) 754–4547.
Reservations: (877) 444–6777; www.ReserveUSA.com.
Activities: Fishing, swimming, boating, water-skiing and water sports.
Season: March–October.
Finding the campground: From Interstate 40 take exit 226 and go north on Tennessee Highway 171 for 4.3 miles to U.S. Highway 70. Turn left (west) onto US 70 and go 0.9 mile. Turn right onto Nonaville Road; go 2.4 miles and turn right onto Saundersville Road. Go 2.4 miles to the campground.

The campground: Cedar Creek is located on sort of a peninsula on Old Hickory Lake. The campground is large, very level, and well maintained. There is no designated wheelchair-accessible site, but all the sites are flat. If you like to have room between the sites, this campground will work for you. A day-use area next to the campground provides a boat launch and dock.

4 Shutes Branch

Location: Old Hickory Lake.
Sites: 34.
Facilities: Electric and water hookups, dump station; showers, flush toilets; laundry; playground; tables, grills, fire rings, lantern poles.
Fee: $$–$$$.
Road conditions: Paved.
Management: U.S. Army Corps of Engineers; (615) 754–4847.
Reservations: (877) 444–6777; www.ReserveUSA.com.
Activities: Fishing, boating, water sports.
Season: May–October.
Finding the campground: From Interstate 40 take exit 226 and go north on Tennessee Highway 171 for 4.3 miles to U.S. Highway 70. Turn left (west) onto US 70 and go 0.9 mile. Turn right onto Nonaville Road and go 2.4 miles, and then turn left onto Saundersville Road. Go 3.3 miles and turn left onto Needmore Road. Go 0.2 mile; the campground is on the left.

The campground: Shutes Branch is not located on Old Hickory Lake, but it's on a hillside across the road overlooking Old Hickory. The sites have plenty of space for a family to spread out. A boat launch and dock about a quarter mile from the campground provide access to Old Hickory Lake; the lake itself is within walking distance of the campground.

5 Cedars of Lebanon State Park

Location: South of Lebanon.
Sites: 117.
Facilities: Electric and water hookups, dump station; showers, flush toilets; laundry; swimming pool, playgrounds; tables, grills, fire rings, lantern poles.
Fee: $$.
Road conditions: Paved.
Management: Cedars of Lebanon State Park; (615) 443–2769.
Activities: Swimming, hiking, horseback riding, mountain biking.
Season: Year-round; limited camping in winter.
Finding the campground: From Interstate 40 take the Lebanon exit and go south on U.S. Highway 231 for 6.3 miles. Turn left onto Cedar Forest Road and follow signs; this is also the entrance to the park. Follow this road 0.8 mile to the campground entrance.

The campground: Cedars of Lebanon was named for the dense cedar forest that existed in biblical times, and the reason for this name is apparent everywhere. The campground sites are carved out of the cedar forest. There are two sections to the campground. The sites in the first section are close together, giving the feel of a commercial campground; in section two the sites have more room and privacy.

6 Cook

Location: J. Percy Priest Lake.
Sites: 57.
Facilities: Flush toilets, showers; centrally located drinking water; dump station; laundry; tables, grills, fire rings, lantern poles.
Fee: $$.
Road conditions: Paved.
Management: U.S. Army Corps of Engineers; (615) 889–1096.
Reservations: (877) 444–6777; www.ReserveUSA.com.
Activities: Boating, fishing, swimming, water sports, hiking.
Season: May–September.
Finding the campground: From Interstate 40 take exit 221 and go south on Old Hickory Road for 0.6 mile. Turn left onto Bell Road and go 0.7 mile; turn right onto South New Hope Road and go 1.2 miles. Turn right onto Stewarts Ferry Pike and go 1.5 miles; the campground is on the left.

The campground: The cedar tree is the dominant tree of the landscape here, with most of the sites surrounded by cedars. The cedar trees provide a dense forest between sites, adding privacy for campers. There is a day-use area next to the campground with a fishing pier and boat launch.

7 Seven Points

Location: J. Percy Priest Lake.
Sites: 60.
Facilities: Electric and water hookups, dump station; showers, flush toilets; boat launch, beach; laundry; tables, grills, fire rings, lantern poles.
Fee: $$–$$$.
Road conditions: Paved.
Management: U.S. Army Corps of Engineers; (615) 889–5198.
Reservations: (877) 444–6777; www.ReserveUSA.com.
Activities: Fishing, boating, swimming, water sports.
Season: April–October.
Finding the campground: From Interstate 40 take exit 221 and go south on Old Hickory Road for 0.6 mile. Turn left onto Bell Road and go 0.7 mile. Turn right onto South New Hope Road and go 1.2 miles. Turn left onto Stewarts Ferry Pike and go 1.2 miles; the campground is on the left.

The campground: If you like campgrounds with great waterfront sites, then you're sure to enjoy Seven Points. It's a large, spacious camping area with big sites for campers and RVs. Some of the sites have the normal back-in spot for the RV and also a spot to the side for parking a tow vehicle. The waterfront sites slope gently to the lake, creating a great place to relax near the water. Boats can be moored at the lakeside sites.

8 Long Hunter State Park

Location: J. Percy Priest Lake.
Sites: One large group site.
Facilities: Tables.
Fee: $–$$$.
Road conditions: Paved.
Management: Long Hunter State Park; (615) 885–2422.
Activities: Hiking, canoeing, fishing, boating, water sports, swimming.
Season: Year-round.
Finding the campground: From Interstate 40 take exit 226 and go south on Tennessee Highway 171 for 6.8 miles. Turn at the sign for the state park.

The campground: The campground at Long Hunter is for group camping only—scouting groups or church groups, for example. The group must have adult supervision. The camping area is primitive, with no hookups, but it does have picnic tables. There are lots of activities for groups to do: hiking, canoeing, swimming, and fishing, just to name a few. The fee is based on twenty-five persons, with a small extra charge for each additional person.

9 Poole Knobs

Location: J. Percy Priest Lake.
Sites: 90.
Facilities: Electric and water hookups, dump station; showers, flush toilets; laundry; tables, grills, fire rings, lantern poles; boat launch.
Fee: $–$$$.
Road conditions: Paved.
Management: U.S. Army Corps of Engineers; (615) 459–6948.
Reservations: (877) 444–6777; www.ReserveUSA.com.
Activities: Fishing, boating, water sports.
Season: May–September.
Finding the campground: From U.S. Highway 70S (Murfreesboro Pike) in LaVergne, watch for the campground sign and turn onto Fergus Road. Follow Fergus Road 0.8 mile and turn right onto Jones Mill Road. Go 3.9 miles to the campground.

The campground: There are two camping areas at Poole Knobs, so you have a choice of what you like. The first area is near the water, with sites on the lake. Most of the lakeshore is rocky and there is no beach area, so swimming is at your risk. The sites in this section are very nice, with a large camping pad made from timbers and gravel that are perfect for grilling and relaxing on. The other section is away from the lake on a forested hilltop. These wooded sites have the look and feel of being much farther from the big city than they really are. They are just as nice as the sites on the water, but the fee per night is less.

10 Anderson Road

Location: J. Percy Priest Lake.
Sites: 37.
Facilities: Showers, flush toilets; centrally located drinking water; dump station; laundry; boat launch, beach; tables, grills.
Fee: $$.
Road conditions: Paved.
Management: U.S. Army Corps of Engineers; (615) 361–1980.
Reservations: (877) 444–6777; www.ReserveUSA.com.
Activities: Fishing, boating, swimming, hiking, water sports.
Season: May–September.
Finding the campground: From Interstate 40 exit 219, take Stewarts Ferry Pike south; Stewarts Ferry Pike becomes Bell Road at the first traffic light. Stay on Bell Road 4.7 miles and then turn left onto Smith Springs Road. Go 1.1 miles and turn left onto Anderson Road and go 1.3 miles to the campground entrance. There are signs most of the way.

The campground: Anderson Road Campground is more primitive than some of the other campgrounds on J. Percy Priest Lake; it has no electric or water hookups. If you're OK with not having that, this is a very nice camping area. There are large spaces between most of the sites—great for having a feeling of seclusion. Some sites are waterfront and others are in the cedar trees away from the lake. A nearby recreation area provides a boat launch, beach area, and hiking trails.

11 Cheatham Dam

Location: Cumberland River–Ashland City.
Sites: 45.
Facilities: Electric and water hookups, dump station; showers, flush toilets; laundry; playground, boat launch; tables, grills, lantern poles.
Fee: $$.
Road conditions: Paved.
Management: U.S. Army Corps of Engineers; (615) 792–3715.
Reservations: (877) 444–6777; www.ReserveUSA.com.
Activities: Fishing, boating, hiking, tennis courts.
Season: April–October.
Finding the campground: From the junction of Tennessee Highways 49 and 12 in Ashland City, take TN 12 north for 8.5 miles. Turn left onto Cheatham Dam Road and go 2.9 miles; the campground is on the left.

The campground: Relaxing on the banks of the Cumberland River is what comes to mind when I think about Cheatham Dam Campground. This is a wonderful camping area along the banks of the river, with large hardwood shade trees adding to the relaxing atmosphere. Large RV sites, plenty of grassy areas, tennis courts, and a nearby beach make this a great place for the family to camp.

12 Harpeth River Bridge

Location: Harpeth River–Ashland City.
Sites: 15.
Facilities: Tables, grills, fire rings, lantern poles; boat launch; volleyball, playground.
Fee: $.
Road conditions: Paved.
Management: U.S. Army Corps of Engineers; (615) 792-4195.
Activities: Canoeing, fishing.
Season: May–October.
Finding the campground: From the junction of Tennessee Highways 49 and 12 in Ashland City, take TN 49 west for 5 miles. Watch for the sign; the campground is on the right before you cross the bridge.

The campground: The Harpeth River Bridge Campground is rather small and primitive but very clean and well kept. It is located on sort of an island, with water on two sides—on one side is the easy-flowing river and on the other is a backwater area; both are good fishing spots. The sites are big and will hold a large RV even though there are no hookups. This is a great spot for basing a canoe trip on the lower section of the Harpeth River.

Area 4

Land Between the Lakes National Recreation Area

Land Between the Lakes is a 170,000-acre National Recreation Area approximately 90 miles north of Nashville. It is the largest inland peninsula in the United States, stretching into both Tennessee and Kentucky. Formed when the Tennessee and Cumberland Rivers were impounded, creating Kentucky Lake and Lake Barkley, LBL was designated a National Recreation Area in 1963 by President John F. Kennedy. Today it receives an average two million visitors a year.

The popularity of Land Between the Lakes is easy to understand; there's something here for everyone who enjoys the great outdoors. Boating, fishing, hiking, horseback riding, swimming, bicycling, and wildlife viewing are a few of the outdoor activities available at LBL. Visitors can also see a working 1800s farm at the Homeplace Living History Farm, view the stars at the Golden Pond Planetarium, or learn more about the area at the Woodlands Nature Center. During the winter months bald eagles can be spotted at LBL; some years as many as 150 eagles migrate here from northern areas. Elk and bison can be viewed year-round at the Elk and Bison Prairie.

There are camping opportunities at Land Between the Lakes in both Tennessee and Kentucky, but in this guide I have listed only the ones in Tennessee.

For more information:

Land Between the Lakes
100 Van Morgan Drive
Golden Pond, KY 42211-9001
(270) 924-2000
(800) LBL-7077
www.lbl.org

1 Piney

Location: Land Between the Lakes, Kentucky Lake.
Sites: 383.
Facilities: Electric, water, and sewer hookups, dump station; showers, flush toilets; laundry; boat launch, beach; tables, lantern poles, fire rings, grills.
Fee: $$–$$$.
Road conditions: Paved.
Management: USDA Forest Service; (931) 232-5331.
Activities: Fishing, hunting, hiking, boating, water sports, swimming, bicycling, wildlife viewing.
Season: March–November.

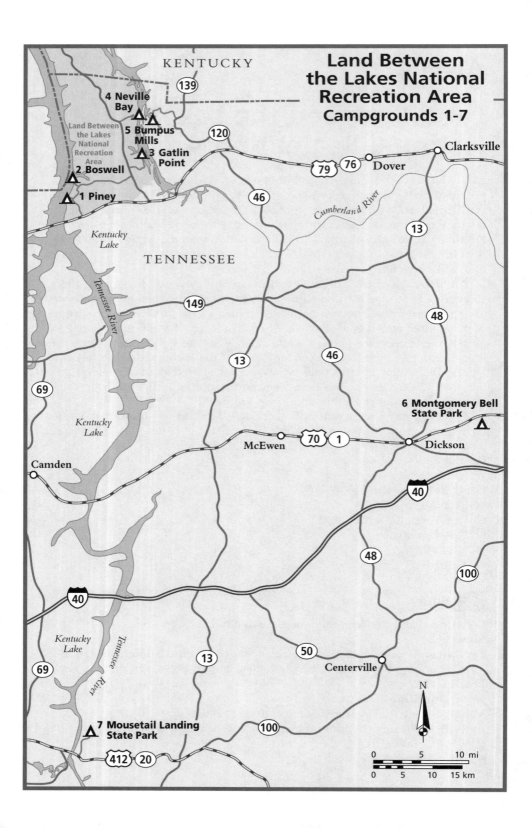

Land Between the Lakes National Recreation Area
Campgrounds 1-7

KENTUCKY

139

4 Neville Bay

Land Between the Lakes National Recreation Area

5 Bumpus Mills

3 Gatlin Point

120

2 Boswell

1 Piney

Clarksville

79 76 Dover

46

Cumberland River

13

Kentucky Lake

TENNESSEE

Tennessee River

149

48

69

13

46

Kentucky Lake

6 Montgomery Bell State Park

McEwen

70 1

Dickson

Camden

40

48

100

40

Kentucky Lake

Tennessee River

69

13

50

Centerville

N

7 Mousetail Landing State Park

100

412 20

100

0   5   10 mi
0   5   10   15 km

	Group sites	RV sites	Total sites	Max. RV length	Hookups	Toilets	Showers	Drinking water	Dump station	Pets	Wheelchair	Recreation	Fee($)	Season	Can reserve	Stay limit
1 Piney		324	383	40	EWS	F	•	•	•	•	•	FSHBLW	$$–$$$	Mar–Nov.		21
2 Boswell			22	30		V		•		•		FSBLW	$			14
3 Gatlin Point		18	18	25		V		•		•		FBLW	$			14
4 Neville Bay			5			V						LB				14
5 Bumpus Mills		21	33	45	EW	F	•	•	•	•		BFSL	$$	May–Sept.	•	14
6 Montgomery Bell State Park		75	119	32	E	F	•	•	•	•	•	BCLHFS	$$			14
7 Mousetail Landing State Park		19	25	40	EW	FV	•	•	•	•	•	SFBLHW	$$			14

Hookups: W = Water E = Electric S = Sewer **Toilets:** F = Flush V = Vault P = Pit C = Chemical **Recreation:** H = Hiking S = Swimming F = Fishing B = Boating L = Boat Launch R = Horseback Riding O = Off-highway driving W = Wildlife watching M = Mountain Biking C = Canoeing G = Golf K = Kayaking **Maximum Trailer/RV length** given in feet. **Stay Limit** given in days. **Fee** given in dollars. If no entry under **Season,** campground is open all year. If no entry under **Fee,** camping is free.

Finding the campground: From Dover take U.S. Highway 79 south approximately 12 miles. Turn right onto Fort Henry Road and go 2.5 miles; turn left at the campground sign and go 0.2 mile to entrance.

The campground: Piney is the cream of the campground crop at Land Between the Lakes in Tennessee. This campground has about everything you could want, but it is very large—with 383 sites, one of the biggest in the state. The drawback is that there are lots of people camping here, so seclusion is not on top of the list of amenities. Piney is on the shores of Kentucky Lake (Tennessee River), and its location is very scenic. For a large campground, it is very clean and well managed. Most of the sites are level and shaded by hardwood trees. For the person wanting the camping experience without camping, Piney has nine primitive camping shelters. The cabins are one room and sleep four with a double bed and a bunk bed. The shelters can be reserved by calling (270) 924-2044.

2 Boswell

Location: Land Between the Lakes, Kentucky Lake.
Sites: 22.
Facilities: Centrally located water; vault toilets; boat launch; tables, grills, fire rings.
Fee: $.
Road conditions: Paved and gravel.
Management: USDA Forest Service; (270) 924-2000.
Activities: Fishing, hunting, hiking, boating, water sports, wildlife viewing.
Season: Year-round.
Finding the campground: From Dover take U.S. Highway 79 south approx-

imately 12 miles. Turn right onto Fort Henry Road; go 4.5 miles and turn left onto Forest Road 232. Go 1.8 miles to the campground. FR 232 becomes a gravel road, but is in good shape and easily traveled.

The campground: Boswell is a more primitive camping experience on Kentucky Lake. There are no hookups and the sites do not have paved parking areas, but a small RV could park here. The sites are on a small rise overlooking Kentucky Lake. Boswell is not far from Piney on the same section of lake but gets fewer visitors because it's farther from the main road and has fewer amenities. It's a choice of what kind of camping you're looking for.

3 Gatlin Point

Location: Land Between the Lakes, Lake Barkley.
Sites: 18.
Facilities: Centrally located water; tables, grills, fire rings; boat launch.
Fee: $.
Road conditions: Gravel; some places narrow and rough.
Management: USDA Forest Service; (270) 924–2000.
Activities: Fishing, hunting, boating, water sports, wildlife viewing, hiking.
Season: Year-round.
Finding the campground: From Dover take U.S. Highway 79 south approximately 5 miles. Watch for the sign and turn right onto The Trace. Follow The Trace 4.7 miles and turn right onto Forest Road 227 (FR 227 is gravel). Follow FR 227 approximately 4 miles; the campground is on the left. Alternate route: Just after the turning onto FR 227, at 0.7 mile, Forest Road 228 turns left. This is a shorter way to Gatlin Point Campground, but it is narrow and rough.

The campground: Gatlin Point is a lot like Boswell Campground, but I liked Gatlin Point a little better. The parking sites are level and very shaded, and the section of Lake Barkley where it is located seems more peaceful. All the sites are primitive, with no hookups. About a quarter mile from the campground is a bridge across the lake; this seems to be a good fishing spot, and we also spotted a bald eagle from here. For the person looking to get away from the crowds but still have a clean, organized campground, this is the place.

4 Neville Bay

Location: Land Between the Lakes, Lake Barkley.
Sites: 5.
Facilities: Tables; vault toilets.
Fee: Free.
Road conditions: Paved and gravel.
Management: USDA Forest Service; (270) 924–2000.
Activities: Fishing, hunting, boating, hiking, water sports, wildlife viewing.
Season: Year-round.
Finding the campground: From Dover take U.S. Highway 79 south approx-

Tent site at Land Between the Lakes

imately 5 miles. Watch for the sign and turn right onto The Trace; follow The Trace 9.8 miles and turn right onto Forest Road 214. Go 1.5 miles to Neville Bay. FR 214 is gravel but smooth and fairly wide.

The campground: Neville is basically a lake-access area, but camping is allowed here. There are no marked sites, just an open grassy area with five picnic tables. When I visited, it was clean. No one was camping, and it appeared that the area doesn't get used much for camping.

5 Bumpus Mills

Location: Lake Barkley.
Sites: 33.
Facilities: Electric and water hookups, dump station; showers, flush toilets; playground; boat launch; tables, grills.
Fee: $$.
Road conditions: Paved.
Management: U.S. Army Corps of Engineers; (931) 232–8831.

Reservations: (877) 444–6777; www.ReserveUSA.com.
Activities: Fishing, boating, water sports, swimming.
Season: May–September.
Finding the campground: From Dover take U.S. Highway 79 south approximately 3 miles and turn right at campground sign onto Tennessee Highway 120 north. Go 10 miles and turn left onto Tobaccoport Road; go 2.8 miles and turn left onto Oak Hill Road. Go 0.9 mile and turn left onto Forest Road; go 0.2 mile to the campground entrance.

The campground: Bumpus Mills is a medium-size campground located in a beautiful setting of rolling hills next to Lake Barkley. The wooded sites are fairly good sized, fitting most RVs. The campground has a nearby convenience store and public marina.

6 Montgomery Bell State Park

Location: West of Nashville.
Sites: 119.
Facilities: Electric hookups, dump station; showers, flush toilets; playground; tables, grills, fire rings; centrally located drinking water (no water hookups).
Fee: $$.
Road conditions: Paved.
Management: Montgomery Bell State Park; (615) 797–9052.
Activities: Boating, fishing, canoeing, hiking, swimming, tennis, basketball, volleyball.
Season: Year-round.
Finding the campground: From the junction of U.S. Highway 70 and Tennessee Highway 96 in Dickson, take US 70 east 3.7 miles. Watch for the sign; the park entrance is on the right. Follow the signs to the campground.

The campground: As with most of the other state park campgrounds, this one is very nice. The sites vary from large RV spots to small walk-in tent sites. Park information states the maximum RV length to be 32 feet; some of the sites will hold much larger units, and I saw a couple on the day I visited. A small stream runs through the campground, and some of the sites are next to it; these seem to be very popular. Inside the park are three small lakes that provide opportunities for fishing and canoeing without the hassle of large motorboats. The park also has a very nice inn and restaurant. I was very impressed with the wheelchair-accessible sites; they rank near the top of the list of the best I have seen.

7 Mousetail Landing State Park

Location: Tennessee River/Kentucky Lake, east of Parsons.
Sites: 25.
Facilities: Electric and water hookups, dump station; showers, flush toilets; laundry; boat launch; tables, grills, fire rings, lantern poles.
Fee: $$.

Road conditions: Paved.
Management: Mousetail Landing State Park; (901) 847–0841.
Activities: Boating, fishing, hiking, swimming, wildlife watching, volleyball, basketball, archery range.
Season: Year-round.
Finding the campground: From the junction of U.S. Highway 412 and Tennessee Highway 69 in Parsons, take US 412 east approximately 6.5 miles. Turn left onto Tennessee Highway 438 east and go 2.5 miles; watch for the sign. The park entrance is on the left; follow signs to the campground.

The campground: There are two different camping areas at Mousetail Landing State Park. The main campground has twenty-five sites on a ridgetop above the river. These are more developed sites, with electric and water hookups. The sites in this section are good size with enough room for an RV and a second vehicle. Several of these sites appear to be new. The second camping area is known as the primitive area because the sites lack any sort of hookups. The sixteen primitive sites are next to the Tennessee River and have a boat launch. The primitive sites are as nice as the main campground, with large paved parking areas and plenty of room. The entrance to the primitive area is about 1.5 miles before you reach the main entrance. It is worth noting that the road drops off at this turn; caution is in order if you're pulling a low-clearance trailer.

Area 5

Shelbyville, Tim's Ford Lake, and Normandy Lake

The town of Shelbyville is famous for the Tennessee Walking Horse and is home to the Tennessee Walking Horse Celebration. This eleven-day event takes place annually in August. The celebration draws thousands of people each year, from Tennessee and abroad, who delight in the beauty of the Tennessee Walking Horse. Nearby Lynchburg, a small town perhaps better known as the home of the Jack Daniel's Distillery, is also the location of the Tennessee Walking Horse Museum.

Tim's Ford Lake, covering 11,950 acres, is one of the most picturesque lakes in Tennessee. It is a popular fishing destination for many anglers, with catches of smallmouth bass, walleye, crappie, and many other species. Tim's Ford is also a favorite spot in summer for people who enjoy water-related activities.

Normandy Dam, which creates Normandy Lake, is the largest non-power-generating TVA dam on any Tennessee River tributary. Normandy Dam was built in the midseventies as a way of controlling floods, producing a water supply, and creating recreational opportunities. The dam also supplies water to the Normandy Fish Hatchery, one of the largest in the state. There are more than 500 species of fish in Normandy Lake.

For more information:

Shelbyville–Bedford County Chamber of Commerce
100 North Cannon Boulevard
Shelbyville, TN 37160
(931) 684–3482
www.shelbyvilletn.com

Tim's Ford Lake information:
(800) 238–2264

Normandy Lake information:
www.tva.gov/sites/normandy.htm

1 Henry Horton State Park

Location: Northwest of Shelbyville.
Sites: 75.
Facilities: Electric and water hookups, dump station; showers, flush toilets; tables, grills, fire rings, playground.
Fee: $–$$.
Road conditions: Paved and smooth gravel.

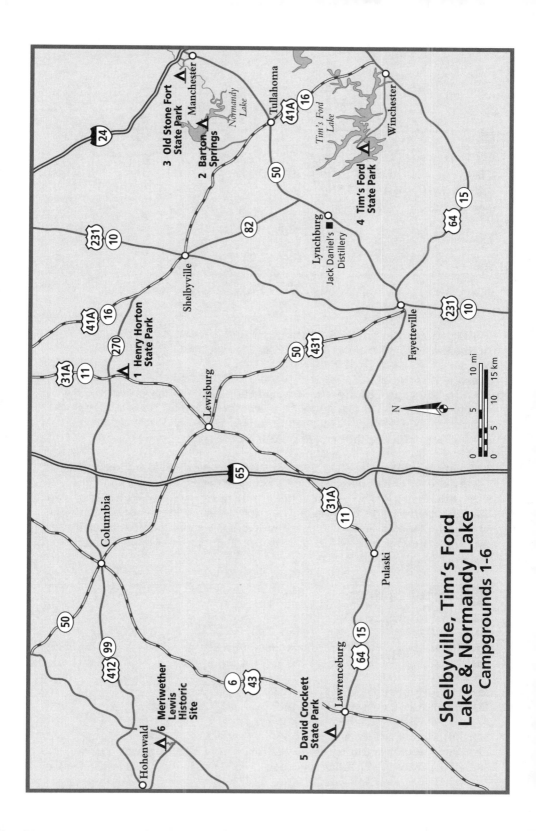

Shelbyville, Tim's Ford
Lake & Normandy Lake
Campgrounds 1-6

1 Henry Horton State Park
2 Barton Springs
3 Old Stone Fort State Park
4 Tim's Ford State Park
5 David Crockett State Park
6 Meriwether Lewis Historic Site

Hohenwald
Columbia
Lewisburg
Shelbyville
Manchester
Tullahoma
Winchester
Fayetteville
Pulaski
Lawrenceburg

Normandy Lake
Tim's Ford Lake
Jack Daniel's Distillery
Lynchburg

0   5   10 mi
0   5   10   15 km

N

	Group sites	RV sites	Total sites	Max. RV length	Hookups	Toilets	Showers	Drinking water	Dump station	Pets	Wheelchair	Recreation	Fee ($)	Season	Can reserve	Stay limit
1 Henry Horton State Park	•	54	75	40	EW	F	•	•	•	•	•	HSGC	$-$$			14
2 Barton Springs		30	69	36	EW	F	•	•	•	•	•	SBFL	$$	March–Oct.		21
3 Old Stone Fort State Park	•	51	51	40	EW	F	•	•	•	•		HCF	$$			14
4 Tim's Ford State Park		50	50	36	EW	F	•	•	•	•	•	FHSGBL	$$			14
5 David Crockett State Park	•	108	108	40	EW	F	•	•	•	•	•	HSFB	$$			14
6 Meriwether Lewis Historic Site		31	31	36		F		•		•	•	H				14

Hookups: W = Water E = Electric S = Sewer **Toilets:** F = Flush V = Vault P = Pit C = Chemical **Recreation:** H = Hiking S = Swimming F = Fishing B = Boating L = Boat Launch R = Horseback Riding O = Off-highway driving W = Wildlife watching M = Mountain Biking C = Canoeing G = Golf K = Kayaking **Maximum Trailer/RV length** given in feet. **Stay Limit** given in days. **Fee** given in dollars. If no entry under **Season,** campground is open all year. If no entry under **Fee,** camping is free.

Management: Henry Horton State Park; (931) 364–2222.
Activities: Hiking, fishing, canoeing, golf, skeet shooting, volleyball, swimming.
Season: Year-round.
Finding the campground: From the junction of U.S. Highways 231 and 41A in Shelbyville, take US 41A north 7.2 miles. Turn left onto Tennessee Highway 270 west and go 9.5 miles; turn left onto U.S. Highway 31A south and go 0.7 mile. The entrance to the campground is on the right.

The campground: The sites at Henry Horton are divided into two groups: twenty-one primitive sites with no electric or water hookups and fifty-four sites with hookups. The road into the primitive area is graveled but smooth. I like the primitive sites because they are spaced out, with plenty of room. The sites in the modern area have paved pull-in sites; some are pull-through sites that are posted for RVs 28 feet or longer. A golf course, skeet-shooting range, and swimming pool are nearby.

2 Barton Springs

Location: Normandy Lake.
Sites: 69.
Facilities: Electric and water hookups, dump station; showers, flush toilets; boat launch; tables, grills.
Fee: $$.
Road conditions: Paved.
Management: Tennessee Valley Authority; (931) 857–9222.
Activities: Fishing, boating, water sports.
Season: March–October.
Finding the campground: From the junction of U.S. Highway 41 and Tennessee Highway 269 in Tullahoma, take TN 269 north; this route is also known

Old dam on Duck River, Old Stone Fort State Park

as Normandy Road West. Go 5.2 miles and turn right, crossing the railroad tracks. After crossing the railroad tracks, bear left. There is no sign, but this is Frank Hiles Road; follow this 3 miles to the campground on the left.

The campground: This is a great summertime spot for camping next to the water. Located on the shores of Normandy Lake, this medium-size campground is perfectly located for anyone who enjoys fishing, boating, and water sports. There is good fishing here on the lake and good trout fishing at the base of Normandy Dam, where the waters are stocked.

3 | Old Stone Fort State Park

Location: Manchester.
Sites: 51.
Facilities: Electric and water hookups, dump station; showers, flush toilets; tables, grills, fire rings.
Fee: $$.
Road conditions: Paved.
Management: Old Stone Fort State Park; (615) 723–5073.
Activities: Hiking, fishing, golf, tennis.
Season: Year-round.
Finding the campground: From Interstate 24 in Manchester take exit 110 and go south on Tennessee Highway 53 for 0.9 mile. Turn right onto U.S. Highway 41N and go 0.7 mile. The park entrance is on the left; follow the signs to the campground.

The campground: The road leading into the campground crosses the Duck River, and one of the first things you notice is the beauty of the river and surrounding area. Old Stone Fort is a 2,000-year-old Native American ceremonial site that is fascinating to explore. A series of waterfalls on the Duck River draws both sightseers and photographers. Many of the campsites are located on the banks overlooking the river; all are spaced out with plenty of room and privacy.

4 Tim's Ford State Park

Location: Tim's Ford Lake.
Sites: 50.
Facilities: Electric and water hookups, dump station; showers, flush toilets; laundry; boat launch; tables, fire rings, grills.
Fee: $$.
Road conditions: Paved.
Management: Tim's Ford State Park; (615) 967–4457.
Activities: Boating, fishing, hiking, bicycling, golf, swimming.
Season: Year-round.
Finding the campground: From the junction of Tennessee Highways 50 and 130 in Winchester, take TN 50 west 5.1 miles and turn right onto Mansford Road. Go 4.8 miles. The park entrance is on the left; follow the signs to the campground.

The campground: Tim's Ford State Park is located on the lake of the same name. The park campground is not located on the water but on a ridgetop above the lake, set in among the hardwood trees. Camping is enjoyed here year-round, but it was especially beautiful when I visited in the fall. The paved spots for RVs are not as large as at some of the other parks but can still accommodate a 36-foot RV. This area is well known for the lake and fishing, but the park also offers 5 miles of paved trails for bicyclists and hikers, as well as one of the largest swimming pools in the park system, a marina, a bait shop, and rental boats.

5 David Crockett State Park

Location: Lawrenceburg.
Sites: 108.
Facilities: Electric and water hookups, dump station; showers, flush toilets; tables, grills, fire rings.
Fee: $$.
Road conditions: Paved.
Management: David Crockett State Park; (615) 762–9408.
Activities: Hiking, fishing, swimming, outdoor classroom, boating.
Season: Year-round.
Finding the campground: From the junction of U.S. Highways 64 and 43 in Lawrenceburg, take US 64 west 1.4 miles. The park entrance is on the right; follow the signs to the campground.

The campground: Tennessee has two state parks named after David Crockett; the one mentioned earlier in this book is his birthplace, and this one is where he moved his family as an adult and set up his own business. At this location he established a powder mill, gristmill, and distillery on Shoal Creek—all of which were washed away by a flood in 1817. I enjoyed the campground here; its beautiful hilltop setting with plenty of shade is a great spot to camp in summer. The large sites are arranged in a way that makes it easy to park a large RV. Boats can be rented at forty-acre Lindsey Lake for fishing or just relaxing. The park also contains a restaurant and an outdoor classroom for learning more about the environment.

6 Meriwether Lewis Historic Site

Location: Natchez Trace Parkway.
Sites: 31.
Facilities: Flush toilets; tables, grills, fire rings; centrally located water.
Fee: Free.
Road conditions: Paved.
Management: National Park Service; (800) 305–7417.
Activities: Hiking, historic learning.
Season: Year-round.
Finding the campground: The campground is located near mile marker 386 on the Natchez Trace Parkway, at the Meriwether Lewis Historic Site. If you're coming from Hohenwald, take Tennessee Highway 20 east 7 miles to the parkway; the campground is at the junction of TN 20 and the parkway.

The campground: This is a simple, primitive camping area with no hookups. However, it is a good place to spend the night if you're traveling the Natchez Trace Parkway and do not wish to wander far off the road. Don't be fooled by this being a primitive campground, though; it's very orderly and well kept—located on the top of beautiful rolling ridges beneath a canopy of hardwood trees. There are a few pull-through sites, and most will accommodate a 36-foot RV. Its location next to the site of Meriwether Lewis's grave and the place where he came to his untimely death make this a fascinating area for exploring a piece of American history.

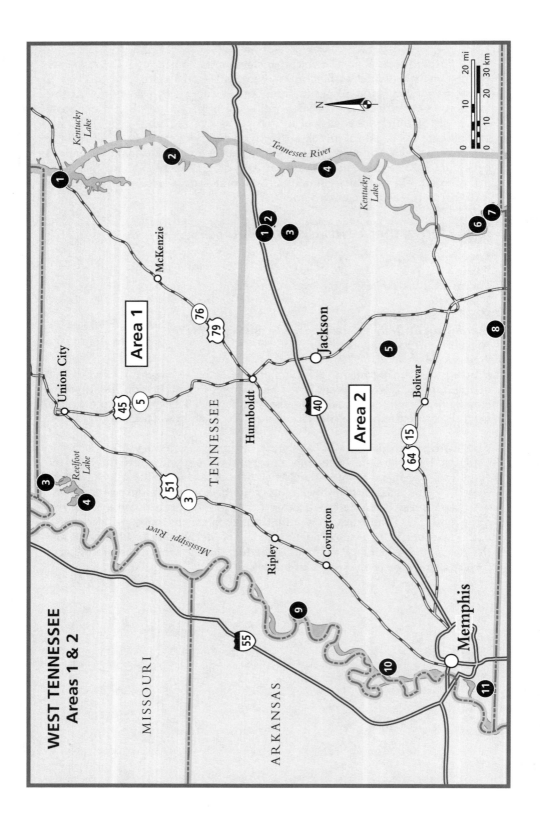

West Tennessee

Area 1

Reelfoot Lake and Kentucky Lake

Reelfoot Lake is a truly amazing place, and the way it was created is equally impressive. An earthquake that shook the Mississippi River Valley in 1811 created a depression that soon filled with water, forming the lake we now know as Reelfoot. Today the lake is both an important wetland area for waterfowl and wildlife and a recreation area for visitors. Thousands of ducks and geese winter here each year, but Reelfoot is best known for its winter bald eagle population. Each year 100 to 200 bald eagles migrate from northern states to Reelfoot to spend the winter. Eagle tours are conducted at several locations during the winter months. Reelfoot is also a popular hunting and fishing area that first drew such hunters as Jim Bowie and Davy Crockett.

Kentucky Lake is the largest man-made lake in the eastern United States and one of the largest in the entire country. Its 160,000 acres of water and more than 2,000 miles of shoreline make it a premier outdoor playground and recreational area. The lake was created when TVA built a dam on the Tennessee River in Kentucky to control flooding on the lower Ohio and Mississippi Rivers; the resulting lake is a mecca for fishing and other water recreation. Although the dam is located in Kentucky, the lake itself stretches from Kentucky south halfway across Tennessee.

For more information:

Northwest Tennessee Tourism
P.O. Box 807
Paris, TN 38242
(866) 698–6386
www.kentuckylaketourism.com
www.reelfootlakeoutdoors.com

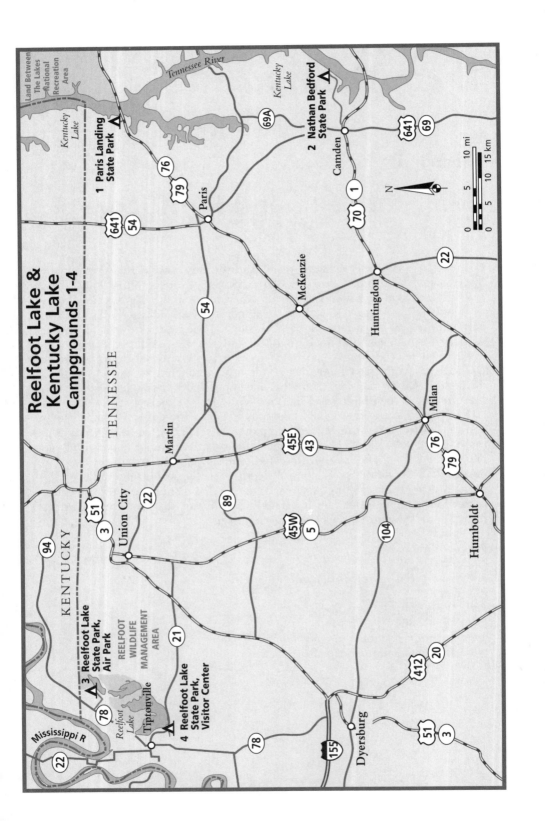

Reelfoot Lake & Kentucky Lake Campgrounds 1-4

1 Paris Landing State Park

2 Nathan Bedford State Park

3 Reelfoot Lake State Park, Air Park

4 Reelfoot Lake State Park, Visitor Center

KENTUCKY

TENNESSEE

Land Between The Lakes National Recreation Area

Tennessee River

Kentucky Lake

REELFOOT WILDLIFE MANAGEMENT AREA

Reelfoot Lake

Mississippi R

Tiptonville

Union City

Martin

Paris

Camden

McKenzie

Huntingdon

Milan

Humboldt

Dyersburg

N

0   5   10 mi
0   5   10   15 km

	Group sites	RV sites	Total sites	Max. RV length	Hookups	Toilets	Showers	Drinking water	Dump station	Pets	Wheelchair	Recreation	Fee ($)	Season	Can reserve	Stay limit
1 Paris Landing State Park		45	63	36	EW	F	•	•	•	•	•	HFSBG	$-$$			14
2 Nathan Bedford State Park	•	53	53	40	EW	F	•	•	•	•	•	HFSB	$$			14
3 Reelfoot Lake State Park—Air Park		14	14	36	EW	F	•	•	•	•	•	FHBW	$$			14
4 Reelfoot Lake State Park—Visitor Center		86	86	36	EW	F	•	•	•	•	•	FHBW	$$	March–Nov.		14

Hookups: W = Water E = Electric S = Sewer **Toilets:** F = Flush V = Vault P = Pit C = Chemical **Recreation:** H = Hiking S = Swimming F = Fishing B = Boating L = Boat Launch R = Horseback riding O = Off-highway driving W = Wildlife watching M = Mountain biking C = Canoeing G = Golf K = Kayaking **Maximum Trailer/RV length** given in feet. **Stay Limit** given in days. **Fee** given in dollars. If no entry under **Season,** campground is open all year. If no entry under **Fee,** camping is free.

1 Paris Landing State Park

Location: Kentucky Lake.
Sites: 63.
Facilities: Water and electric hookups, dump station; showers, flush toilets; laundry; boat launch, swimming pool, restaurant; tables, grills, fire rings, lantern poles.
Fee: $-$$.
Road conditions: Paved.
Management: Paris Landing State Park; (731) 641–4465.
Activities: Fishing, hiking, swimming, golf, boating, water sports.
Season: Year-round.
Finding the campground: From Paris take U.S. Highway 79 north approximately 16 miles. Just before you cross Kentucky Lake, the entrance to the campground is on the left.

The campground: Paris Landing got its name from its location on the Tennessee River. Where the park is now located was a major steamboat port during the 1800s, bringing supplies to the town of Paris. The landing is now a wonderful recreational area. The beautifully landscaped campground, adjacent to the marina and boat launch area, is divided into two sections: an eighteen-site primitive area that offers basic camping and a forty-five-site area with paved sites and hookups. A short distance on the other side of TN 79 is the rest of the park, with a swimming pool, golf course, and restaurant.

2 Nathan Bedford State Park

Location: Kentucky Lake.
Sites: 53.

Fisherman leaving the dock, Paris Landing State Park

Facilities: Water and electric hookups, dump station; showers, flush toilets; boat launch; tables, grills.
Fee: $$.
Road conditions: Paved.
Management: Nathan Bedford State Park; (731) 584–6356.
Activities: Hiking, swimming, fishing, boating, water sports.
Season: Year-round.
Finding the campground: From the junction of U.S. Highways 70 and 641 in Camden, take US 70 east 1 mile to Tennessee Highway 191. Take TN 191 north through downtown, following the signs 7.9 miles to the park entrance.

The campground: The main campground at Nathan Bedford is situated between two hills in a quiet hollow known as Happy Hollow. A small stream flows through the campground. The sites vary from walk-in sites to large RV sites, with the largest able to hold a 40-foot RV. Some sites are on a slight hillside; the ones near the bottom of the hollow are more level and have more shade. The other camping area is a short distance away on the shores of Kentucky Lake. None of the fifteen sites here has hookups, but there is centrally located water. These sites are large and level. The boat launch is very near here.

3 Reelfoot Lake State Park—Air Park

Location: Reelfoot Lake.
Sites: 14.
Facilities: Water and electric hookups, dump station; showers, flush toilets; tables, grills.
Fee: $$.
Road conditions: Paved.
Management: Reelfoot Lake State Park; (731) 253–7756.
Activities: Hiking, boating, fishing, hunting, eagle watching.
Season: Year-round.
Finding the campground: From the junction of Tennessee Highways 78 and 21 in Tiptonville, take TN 78 north 7.7 miles and turn right onto Tennessee Highway 213 east. Go 3.2 miles; the road ends at the campground.

The campground: The Air Park Campground gets its name from the fact that it is located next to a small landing strip. The landing strip is not that busy and doesn't really disturb the campground. The campground is also next to the Air Park Inn and Restaurant at Reelfoot Lake. The campground is very open, with mostly small trees for shade and lots of grassy areas for kids to play. This is not a wilderness experience, but it's a good location for accessing the lake and watching the eagles. There is a boat launch just off TN 213, about 2 miles from the campground.

4 Reelfoot Lake State Park—Visitor Center

Location: Reelfoot Lake.
Sites: 86.
Facilities: Water and electric hookups, dump station; showers, flush toilets; laundry; boat launch, tables, grills.
Fee: $$.
Road conditions: Paved.
Management: Reelfoot Lake State Park; (731) 253–7756.
Activities: Fishing, hiking, boating, eagle watching.
Season: March–November.
Finding the campground: From the junction of Tennessee Highways 78 and 21 in Tiptonville, take TN 21 east 5.4 miles; the campground entrance is on the left.

The campground: This campground is located next to the visitor center for Reelfoot Lake State Park. It, too, is not in a wilderness setting but is located near stores and other facilities. It is, however, on the shores of Reelfoot Lake, and despite its location near commercialization it's a very peaceful place to camp and to base a fishing trip. The sites are level with lots of room and shade from large hardwood trees. Fish-cleaning stations are provided throughout the campground, and local guide services are available nearby.

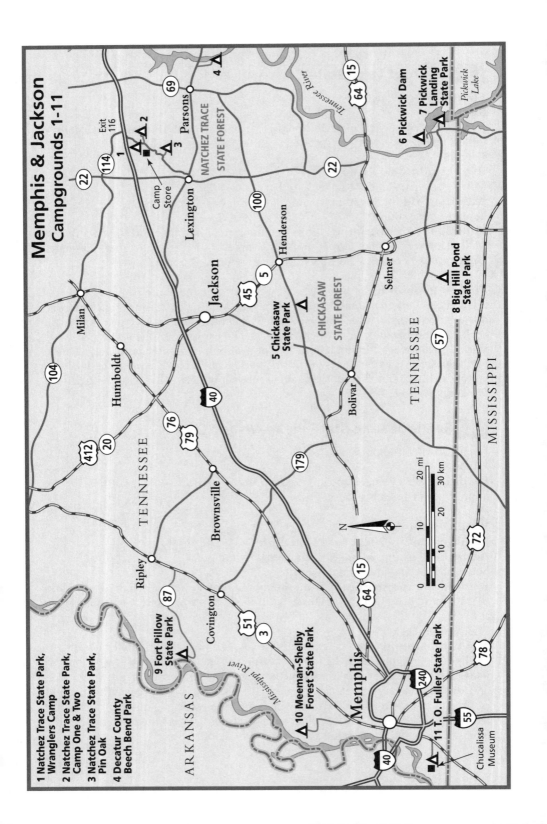

Memphis & Jackson
Campgrounds 1-11

1 Natchez Trace State Park, Wranglers Camp
2 Natchez Trace State Park, Camp One & Two
3 Natchez Trace State Park, Pin Oak
4 Decatur County Beech Bend Park
5 Chickasaw State Park
6 Pickwick Dam
7 Pickwick Landing State Park
8 Big Hill Pond State Park
9 Fort Pillow State Park
10 Meeman-Shelby Forest State Park
11 T. O. Fuller State Park

Area 2

Memphis and Jackson

There are two sizable towns in the southwest corner of Tennessee—Memphis and Jackson, both full of art, culture, and history with an eye on the future. Memphis is located in the very southwest tip of the state, perched on the Chickasaw Bluffs overlooking the mighty Mississippi River. It is bordered by Arkansas and Mississippi on the west and south, respectively. Memphis is the nation's eighteenth largest city and may be best known for its delicious barbecue and as home to the "King of Rock & Roll," Elvis Presley. But it also ranks sixth in the nation for the number of properties on the National Register of Historic Places. Memphis is a city with many influences and styles; there is something here for every taste and interest.

Jackson, Tennessee, a little more than an hour's drive east of Memphis, was first settled in 1818 and named Alexandria. The name was later changed to Jackson in honor of war hero Andrew Jackson, who was later to become our nation's seventh president. Davy Crockett, who traveled around Tennessee extensively, at one time made Jackson his home. It was here in Jackson, after losing his bid for reelection to Congress, that he gave a speech from which one of his most famous quotes came: "You can go to hell, I'm going to Texas." Today Jackson is a growing city of around 107,000 persons, with a diverse cultural base that takes pride in the city's history and looks forward to the future.

For more information:

Memphis Area
Chamber of Commerce
22 North Front Street #200
P.O. Box 224
Memphis, TN 38101
(901) 543–3500
www.memphischamber.com

Jackson Chamber of Commerce
197 Auditorium Street
P.O. Box 1904
Jackson, TN 38302-1904
(731) 423–2200
www.jacksontn.com

Visitor Information Center
Tennessee State Welcome Center
119 North Riverside Drive
Memphis, TN 38101
(901) 543–5333

Note: There are four campgrounds at Natchez Trace State Park. Campgrounds One and Two are next to each other; but the Wranglers and Pin Oak Campgrounds are several miles apart. Therefore I have listed the Wranglers and the Pin Oak Campgrounds separately and Campgrounds One and Two together.

	Group sites	RV sites	Total sites	Max. RV length	Hookups	Toilets	Showers	Drinking water	Dump station	Pets	Wheelchair	Recreation	Fee ($)	Season	Can reserve	Stay limit
1 Natchez Trace State Park—Wranglers Campground		62	62	40	EW	F	•	•	•	•	•	RH	$$			14
2 Natchez Trace State Park—Campgrounds 1 and 2		67	67	35	WE	F	•	•	•	•	•	HFB	$$	Campground 2 Closed in Winter		14
3 Natchez Trace State Park—Pin Oak Campground		77	77	45	EWS	F	•	•		•	•	FHBL	$$			14
4 Decatur County Beech Bend Park		74	74	36	WE	F	•	•	•	•	•	FBLS	$$			NO LIMIT
5 Chickasaw State Park	•	83	112	36	WE	F	•	•	•	•	•	FBSHRMG	$$			14
6 Pickwick Dam		62	92	36	WE	F	•	•	•	•	•	FBL	$$			14
7 Pickwick Landing State Park		48	48	36	WES	F	•	•	•	•	•	FBSHLG	$$			14
8 Big Hill Pond State Park	•	30	30	36		F	•	•			•	FBOHLMR	$$			14
9 Fort Pillow State Park	•	40	40	30		F	•	•		•	•	HFWB	$			14
10 Meeman-Shelby Forest State Park	•	49	49	45	WE	F	•	•	•	•	•	FHS	$$		•	14
11 T. O. Fuller State Park	•	45	45	36	WE	F	•	•	•	•	•	HGS	$$			14

Hookups: W = Water E = Electric S = Sewer **Toilets:** F = Flush V = Vault P = Pit C = Chemical **Recreation:** H = Hiking S = Swimming F = Fishing B = Boating L = Boat Launch R = Horseback Riding O = Off-highway driving W = Wildlife watching M = Mountain Biking C = Canoeing G = Golf K = Kayaking **Maximum Trailer/RV length** given in feet. **Stay Limit** given in days. **Fee** given in dollars. If no entry under **Season,** campground is open all year. If no entry under **Fee,** camping is free.

1 Natchez Trace State Park—Wranglers Campground

Location: East of Jackson.
Sites: 62.
Facilities: Water and electric hookups, dump station; showers, flush toilets; tables, grills, fire rings, lantern poles.
Fee: $$.
Road conditions: Paved.
Management: Natchez Trace State Park; (731) 968–3742.
Activities: Hiking, horseback riding.
Season: Year-round.
Finding the campground: From Interstate 40 take exit 116 and go south on Tennessee Highway 114 for 2.3 miles. The campground entrance is on the right.

The campground: The name of this campground comes from the fact that it is next to the riding stables, and some of the sites have tie-outs for horses. The campground is well spaced into three different areas. Not all sites have the tie-outs, so I recommend getting there early if you need one of these sites.

Campers must clean up after their own horses, which helps maintain a clean camping area. Sites 35 to 62 have more room for a larger RV or trailer. There are nearby lakes for fishing and trails for hiking.

2 | Natchez Trace State Park—Campgrounds One and Two

Location: East of Jackson.
Sites: 67.
Facilities: Water and electric hookups, dump station; showers, flush toilets; tables, grills, lantern poles.
Fee: $$.
Road conditions: Paved; smooth gravel in the campground.
Management: Natchez Trace State Park; (731) 968–3742.
Activities: Fishing, hiking, paddleboats.
Season: Campground One year-round; Campground Two closed in winter.
Finding the campground: From Interstate 40 take exit 116 and go south on Tennessee Highway 114. The road forks at the park store; stay to the left on Parson's Road for a total of 5.5 miles to the entrance to Campgrounds One and Two.

The campground: Both One and Two are nice, clean campgrounds. Campground One is next to Cub Lake, where paddleboats can be rented and fishing is good. Campground One's twenty-three sites all have water and electric hookups. Campground Two is away from the lake, more in the forest. All forty-four sites have water but not all have electric hookups; twenty sites are tent only.

3 | Natchez Trace State Park—Pin Oak Campground

Location: East of Jackson.
Sites: 77.
Facilities: Water, electric, and sewer hookups at all sites; showers, flush toilets; laundry; boat launch; tables, grills, fire rings.
Fee: $$.
Road conditions: Paved.
Management: Natchez Trace State Park; (731) 968–3742.
Activities: Hiking, fishing.
Season: Year-round.
Finding the campground: From Interstate 40 take exit 116 and go south on Tennessee Highway 114. The road forks at the park store; stay to the right on TN 114, also known as Natchez Trace Road, for approximately 7.5 miles. Turn left at the sign for the campground onto an unsigned road and go 2.7 miles to the campground entrance.

The campground: Pin Oak is a new campground situated on a small hill overlooking Pin Oak Lake. This is a great setup for the RV'er. All sites have electric, water, and sewer hookups, but the sites are not just for the RV'er; tent campers are welcome here, too. There is also a beach area and boat launch.

Most of the sites are very large, and some are pull-thoughs. The only drawback is that most of the sites lack shade trees. Most of the sites are on a slight hill, but a few sites are at the water's edge.

4 Decatur County Beech Bend Park

Location: Tennessee River/Kentucky Lake, east of Parsons.
Sites: 74.
Facilities: Water and electric hookups, dump station; showers, flush toilets; boat launch; tables, grills, fire rings, lantern poles.
Fee: $$.
Road conditions: Paved.
Management: Decatur County Parks & Recreation; (731) 847–4252.
Activities: Fishing, boating, swimming, water sports.
Season: Year-round.
Finding the campground: From the junction of Tennessee Highway 69 and U.S. Highway 412 in Parsons, take US 412 east 4.6 miles and turn right onto Tennessee Highway 100W. Go 1.6 miles; the campground entrance is on the left.

The campground: Beech Bend Park is the most well kept campground run by a county department that I have ever visited. This level camping area sits back on a slough just off the main channel of the Tennessee River. There is a boat launch ramp so that campers can take advantage of the good fishing. Reservations are not accepted, and there is no limit on the number of days you can camp.

5 Chickasaw State Park

Location: West of Henderson.
Sites: 112.
Facilities: Water and electric hookups, dump station; showers, flush toilets; beach; tables, grills, fire rings.
Fee: $$.
Road conditions: Paved.
Management: Chickasaw State Park; (731) 989–5141.
Activities: Hiking, fishing, swimming, paddleboats, golf, horseback riding, tennis, basketball.
Season: Year-round; tent camping area closed in winter.
Finding the campground: From the junction of Tennessee Highways 365 and 100 in Henderson, take TN 100 west 8.3 miles. Turn left at the sign for the park entrance and follow the signs to the campground.

The campground: There are three camping areas at Chickasaw State Park, and all three are very close to one another. A twenty-nine-site tent area at the lakeside is closed in winter. These have water but no electric hookups. The sites here are rather secluded, set within the forest with a good feeling of privacy. The riding stables and wranglers camping area are a short distance away.

Thirty-one sites here offer water and electric hookups for RVs. These sites are for those folks who wish to be near their horses. There are more than 100 miles of horseback trails in the Chickasaw State Forest, and you can bring your own horse or hire one from the stables. It's a nice, level area, very open with lots of grass and shaded by tall, majestic pine trees. The RV section, as it is called, is only a few hundred yards away and has fifty-two sites spaced out around a slight hillside. The RV sites have water and electric hookups and even though they are called RV sites, tents are welcome. All three areas are within walking distance of one another and the activities in the park.

6 Pickwick Dam

Location: Tennessee River/Pickwick Lake.
Sites: 92.
Facilities: Water and electric hookups, dump station; showers, flush toilets; boat launch; tables, grills, fire rings, lantern poles.
Fee: $$.
Road conditions: Paved.
Management: Tennessee Valley Authority; (256) 386–2006.
Activities: Fishing, hiking, boating.
Season: Year-round.
Finding the campground: From the junction of Tennessee Highways 45 and 57 in Eastview, take TN 57 east 19 miles. Just after crossing Pickwick Dam, turn left onto Sportsman Road and follow the signs to the campground.

The campground: The campground here is just a few hundred yards downstream from the dam. The sites are not on the banks of the river but just across the road. A boat launch and river access are at the entrance to the campground. The campground is shaded by tall, mature pines trees that litter the ground with pine needles, and give this area a wonderful feel and smell. All the sites are level and will accommodate large RVs or tents; thirty sites have no hookups. There are more recreational opportunities a short distance away at Pickwick Landing State Park.

7 Pickwick Landing State Park

Location: Pickwick Lake/Tennessee River.
Sites: 48.
Facilities: Water, electric, and some sewer hookups, dump station; showers, flush toilets; marina and boat launch; tables, grills, fire rings.
Fee: $$.
Road conditions: Paved.
Management: Pickwick Landing State Park; (800) 250–8615.
Activities: Hiking, fishing, boating and water sports, swimming, golf and tennis.
Season: Year-round.
Finding the campground: From the junction of Tennessee Highways 45 and 57 in Eastview, take TN 57 east 18.2 miles. At the intersection TN 57 turns right; the park entrance is on the left just after this turn.

The campground: Pickwick Landing State Park is one of Tennessee's resort parks, which means that it offers a number of activities for families and individuals. The park has a huge marina, a nice restaurant, and a challenging golf course but also offers such activities as tennis, basketball, and horseshoes. The campground is located within walking distance of the marina, and there are slips available to park private boats. This is a great family campground with something for everyone. Sites are varied in size for both tents and RVs, and some have full hookups.

8 Big Hill Pond State Park

Location: Southeast of Bolivar.
Sites: 30.
Facilities: Showers, flush toilets, centrally located water; boat launch; tables, grills, fire rings.
Fee: $$.
Road conditions: Paved.
Management: Big Hill Pond State Park; (731) 645–7967.
Activities: Hiking, fishing, boating, horseback riding; off-road driving and mountain biking on the back roads.
Season: Year-round.
Finding the campground: From the junction of Tennessee Highways 45 and 57 in Eastview, take TN 57 west 10.7 miles. The park entrance is on the left; follow the signs to the campground.

The campground: This nice, small campground is great for just getting away for a few days. There are no hookups for RVs but it has a modern bathhouse with showers. The sites have plenty of room to pitch a tent and also room for most RVs. The park is named for the thirty-five acre pond that is accessed by a four-wheel-drive road, but not far from the campground is Travis McNatt Lake. This lake is accessed by paved road; there is a boat launch, and private boats are allowed but only small motors.

9 Fort Pillow State Park

Location: Mississippi River.
Sites: 40.
Facilities: Showers, flush toilets, centrally located water; laundry; tables, grills, fire rings.
Fee: $.
Road conditions: Paved.
Management: Fort Pillow State Park; (731) 738–5581.
Activities: Hiking, fishing, wildlife watching, boating.
Season: Year-round.
Finding the campground: From the junction of Tennessee Highway 87 and U.S. Highway 51, take TN 87 west 17.5 miles. Turn right onto Tennessee Highway 207 north and go 1 mile to the park entrance; follow the signs to the campground.

The campground: I really like the campground here; it's a great place to camp while exploring the grounds of the Confederate Fort Pillow. Fort Pillow was originally a Confederate Army fort but was taken by the Union Army, who controlled it for most of the Civil War. This is a fascinating historic area, and I'm anxious to return. The campground here is more primitive, with no hookups, but it does have showers in the bathhouse. The sites are of fair size and work great for tents and smaller RVs; the road through the camp is narrow and could cause problems for very large RVs. There is some good fishing on the fifteen-acre Fort Pillow Lake, which is stocked with bass, bream, crappie, and catfish. A boat launch is provided, but only electric motors are allowed.

10 Meeman-Shelby Forest State Park

Location: Mississippi River.
Sites: 49.
Facilities: Water and electric hookups, dump station; showers, flush toilets; boat launch; tables, grills, fire rings.
Fee: $$.
Road conditions: Paved.
Management: Meeman-Shelby State Park; (901) 876–5215.
Reservations: Reservations are taken for Sites 1 to 6 only; (901) 876–5215.
Activities: Hiking, fishing, bicycling, swimming, disc golf course.
Season: Year-round.
Finding the campground: From Interstate 40 in Memphis take exit 2A and go north on U.S. Highway 51 for 2.7 miles. Turn left onto Tennessee Highway 388N and go 8 miles; turn left onto Locke-Cuba Road and go 0.7 mile. Turn right on Bluff Road; go 0.8 mile and turn left into the park entrance. Follow the signs to the campground.

The campground: This campground provides a great rural escape from the city of Memphis. The road through the campground has been newly repaved and is very wide, making it perfect for RVs. The campground is located on a ridge above the Mississippi River, and a scenic road winds its way from the campground down to the river. Boats can be launched onto the Mississippi here. The park also has two small lakes, Poplar Tree Lake and Piersol Lake. Poplar Tree Lake is 125 acres that regularly has very good catches of fish. Johnboats can be rented, or personal boats can be used on Poplar Tree Lake for a small fee (electric motors only). Reservations are taken on six of the campsites.

11 T. O. Fuller State Park

Location: Memphis City Limits.
Sites: 45.
Facilities: Water and electric hookups, dump station; showers, flush toilets; tables, grills, fire rings, lantern poles.
Fee: $$.

Road conditions: Paved.
Management: T. O. Fuller State Park; (901) 543–7581.
Activities: Hiking, swimming, golf, tennis, basketball, archery range.
Season: Year-round.
Finding the campground: From Interstate 55/240 in Memphis, take exit 7 and go south on U.S. Highway 61 for 1.6 miles. Turn right onto Mitchell Road and go 3.2 miles to the park entrance. Follow the signs to the campground.

The campground: This is the only state park within the city limits of Memphis. The campground here is a great spot for RV'ers wanting to be close to downtown and the tourist sites of Memphis. The sites are large enough to hold just about any size RV, and camping here is peaceful. Once set up in the campground, you would never know that you are as close to Memphis as you are.

About the Author

Growing up in a small, rural East Tennessee town, Harold Stinnette gained an appreciation for nature early in life. As a youth he spent many hours outdoors, fishing with his father or taking trips to the Smokies with his family. As he grew older he became more involved in hiking and camping and eventually developed a desire to record on film the beauty he saw in nature. Harold believes that nature photography is a positive way of learning to protect and preserve the natural world we all share. Harold is well known in Tennessee and throughout the Southeast for his exquisite images of nature and his love of the outdoors. He is a regular speaker at nature events and camera clubs. Sharing nature and nature photography through the teaching of nature photography workshops has been a passion of Harold's for the past twelve years. His images have been published in *Outdoor & Travel Photography*, *Birder's World*, and *Outdoor Photographer* magazines. His photographs have also been featured on postcards and in books and advertisements. Harold lives in Spring City, Tennessee, with his wife, Donna, and son, Brandon, where they own and operate Natural Impressions Nature Photography Workshops and Tours; their Web site is www.NaturalImpressionsphotography.com.